FARM TO TABLE

FARM TO TABLE

Celebrating Stratford Chefs School Alumni,
Recipes & Perth County Producers

ANDREW COPPOLINO

PHOTOS BY TERRY MANZO

Swan Parade
PRESS

In memory of
Lindsay Todd Reid
A talented chef and baker
1966 - 2018

CONTENTS

STRATFORD CHEFS SCHOOL TEAM MEMBERS, RECIPES & PERTH COUNTY PRODUCERS

PREFACE

BY ELEANOR KANE

Looking back to 1983, I would never have imagined that the food scene in this small southwestern Ontario town would have flourished to the extent that we witness today. In that year, the odyssey of the Stratford Chefs School (SCS) began when three restaurateurs, Joe Mandel of The Church, Jim Morris of Rundles, and Eleanor Kane of The Old Prune, hatched a plan to open a chef training program in Stratford, one that would operate during the "off-season" months. With each restaurant's search for qualified kitchen staff, a number of experienced chefs were hired from Europe on a "seasonal" basis, who worked in the intense theatre season trade and then were laid off in the off-season months. There was an obvious logic to establishing a culinary training program to run from November–March, months where chefs turned to teaching, thus retaining much of this talented crew.

From those beginnings, theory classes were taught in what was the Stratford Normal School, right beside the Stratford Festival Theatre; practical classes were taught in the three professional restaurant kitchens, where students were exposed to the reality of working kitchens, in contrast to the larger "demonstration" kitchens found in most community colleges at that time.

From the outset, the distinguishing feature of SCS was, and remains, its "restaurant-focused" training, a cooking school that drew upon the traditions of fine restaurants, of cooking with the finest local and regional products available, of excellent service, and inspired interior design. The Instructors were all working restaurant chefs, drawn from each of the founding restaurants. Neil Baxter, Susan Anderson, Bryan Steele, Chris Woolf, Peter Martin, John Bex, and many others joined as the School evolved; some of this group still teach at SCS today.

Just 10 years after its founding, the SCS hosted Canada's first ever national conference, "Northern Bounty," bringing food professionals from all aspects of the culinary world to Stratford to celebrate the bounty of our land. Five distinct culinary regions were represented from coast to coast: British Columbia, the Prairie provinces, Ontario, Quebec, and the Atlantic provinces. The next "Northern Bounty" conference was held in Vancouver, BC, in 1996, and subsequently in Quebec at Le Château Montebello.

All of this activity enriched the SCS curriculum, and it also created expanded opportunities for its apprentices and graduates across the country. Key figures in Canada's restaurant industry — Sinclair Phillip of Sooke Harbour House, Anne Desjardins of L'Eau à la Bouche, Serge Bruyère of À la Table de Serge Bruyère, Franco Prevedello of Centro — opened their doors and shared their zeal and talents. Canadian food writers and editors such as Elizabeth Baird, Julian Armstrong, James Chatto, and Anita Stewart helped to spread the word about the SCS. Gradually the School welcomed visiting chefs from restaurants around the world — France, Italy, England, Australia, Mexico, the US, Denmark, India, Portugal — to teach for one or two weeks; this created opportunities for graduates to work as stagiaires in some of the world's best restaurants. Gradually, the list of visiting international chefs was matched by a rich lineup of SCS graduates who return to teach at the School, having opened excellent restaurants across the country, and who welcome SCS grads.

In honour of the Stratford Chefs School's 35th anniversary, this cookbook, Farm to Table, showcases alumni chefs whose careers have been shaped and defined by a core practice of the SCS curriculum: the practice of sourcing the finest regional ingredients for a menu, or for a particular dish; ingredients that speak of place, of craft, of environment. The region's farmers and producers are celebrated along with alumni chefs, each side of this equation speaks to a founding principle of the SCS; that of creating strong relationships between chefs and these passionate stewards of our land and waterways. For years, Orientation Day for Level 1 students took place at a farm, Soiled Reputation, on the outskirts of Stratford. In small groups, students foraged for vegetables, greens, and fruits, which became elements of an outdoor luncheon served in the barn. Soiled Reputation owners proudly remain one of the key suppliers to the School. Among others, students are introduced to a leader in animal husbandry, owner of Church Hill Farm Max Lass, who specializes in lamb, pork, and beef of the highest quality, and to cheesemaker Ruth Klahsen at Monforte. They come to understand the symbiotic relationship between the product and the plate.

Farm to Table not only features recipes from some of the region's most celebrated graduates of the Stratford Chefs School, but also includes fascinating interviews with these chefs conducted by CBC food columnist Andrew Coppolino, and striking imagery provided by photographer and SCS alumna Terry Manzo.

Eleanor Kane

STRATFORD CHEFS SCHOOL ALUMNI, RECIPES & PERTH COUNTY PRODUCERS

INTRODUCTION

BY RANDI RUDNER

Welcome to our insight into the lives and kitchens of the chefs at the Stratford Chefs School, and its alumni! Stratford Chefs School is a not-for-profit career college focused on the innovative, hands-on training of high quality aspiring chefs and culinary entrepreneurs.

Since 1983, the core program of Stratford Chefs School has run from late October through early March, and focuses on training culinary apprentices in all aspects of owning and operating a small restaurant.

This culinary apprenticeship program is given in 32 weeks over the course of two years. In Level 1, the students learn the fundamentals of practical cookery and pastry (as well as Front of House service), as well as academic subjects such as food history, food costing, culinary management, sanitation, nutrition, communications, wine, and writing.

In the eight months between Level 1 and Level 2, the students are expected to work in restaurants, to further develop their skill. In Level 2, the students build on their fundamental skills with advanced pastry and larder classes, as well as more detailed courses on gastronomy, business, and restaurant design.

The heart of the Level 2 program is the Dinner Lab program, where the students, under the guidance and supervision of an instructor, work as a team each night to serve dinner to the public. We have different series of dinner labs: a Modern Classics series, to ground the students in the dinner lab format and to reinforce fundamental cooking technique; International Inspirations, where the students try to emulate the menu, style, and service of a restaurant of international renown (such as Eleven Madison Park, The French Laundry, Maison Bras, etc); a Student Designed menu series, where students have the opportunity to execute a menu of their own design; and finally, the Guest Chef Dinner series, where Guest Chefs visiting from across Canada and abroad guide our students in the execution and service of dinner menus that reflect their own cuisine.

Now that the school is comfortably ensconced in its new year-round facility right in Stratford's City Centre, we have the unprecedented opportunity to offer culinary programming right through the spring and summer months, and to serve our wider community. Chef Neil Baxter's weekend cooking class retreats have moved from Rundles to the Chefs School, and offer immersive, hand-on culinary experiences from Friday dinner through Sunday lunch from late March to early May. These classes are suitable for any skill level, from the semi-professional chef to the absolute beginner, and are a great way to meet new people, explore new cuisines, and have a lot of fun!

Open Kitchen at Stratford Chefs School offers recreational cooking classes and culinary workshops for the dedicated home cook. Themes range from explorations of single pieces of equipment (immersion circulators, spiralizers, etc), to investigations into particular cooking methods (bread, fresh pasta, preserving vegetables, ice cream, etc), and even to global cuisines (Indian curry, French country cooking, Spanish tapas, etc). Open Kitchen classes are offered throughout the year, and the schedule varies seasonally.

A word about the recipes: all the recipes in this book are largely exactly as written by their submitting chefs, and so reflect the individual voices of our alumni, some of whom are very chatty, and others of whom are... not. Some recipes are straight to the point and very accessible to the home cook, and some are more discursive, and may be more challenging to execute, requiring multiple components. We hope that you will enjoy meeting these chefs on paper, and discovering what they love about the products of Perth County that they get to work with every day!

randi

LINLEY CONSULTING

Aaron Linley

While it's a stretch to say that the "Wok with Yan" television show inspired him to take up cooking professionally, Stratford Chefs School graduate Aaron Linley still smiles at the thought of the cooking show. "He was a favourite with the funky aprons and the word wok used in humorous ways," the Stratford-born Linley says. "The first recipe I tried at age 12 was one of his." Years later, though, Yan might have helped Linley see that he wasn't interested in university, in fact. "I wanted a tactile job. I started working at Rundles and was intrigued by the lifestyle." The food grabbed him, too. "I still remember eating bouillabaisse, rouille, and the sourdough rolls they used to make. There was an intensity to the flavour. And the kitchen." After six years at Rundles, Linley, who had met and married pastry chef Bronwyn Haver, also an SCS graduate, headed to Halifax on what he calls "an adventure" and worked for Michael Smith before heading to Toronto where the couple learned of a Stratford restaurant willing to sell. "We naively did the deal and said let's see what happens." That was the 2001 birth of Bijou, which they sold in 2015.

Whether in the context of Rundles, Bijou, or his consulting work, Linley says farm-to-table is a natural "list of ingredients" and draws a music analogy: "Working seasonally and locally is just a given. It's like musicians advertising that they're going to play in tune. That would be a strange thing to admit." The concept, he continues, makes good business sense. "Local produce is traditionally less costly and better quality, and Stratford is lucky to have so much to choose from. At Bijou, we had the relationships, and we'd get on the phone and ask what was available." Linley also taught at the school for about eight years and says he loved it. "You can become quite robotic working in a restaurant kitchen. When you turn around and have to explain something in a classroom, you have to think about what you're doing. It's interesting to look at why it's done that way. In many ways, teaching has helped me in my career." Over the course of that career, Linley has found that there are few ambitious kitchens between here and Vancouver that haven't had some contact or connection with the Stratford Chefs School. "There's either a chef who's been to Stratford or has worked with someone who's attended," he says. "My generation of cooks, if they're still cooking, will now be executive chefs across the country. The school has made a mark on them, and they've fostered great ideas at a lot of great restaurants."

LOCO FIELDS

Ryan Bergman

Walking in from his crops, Ryan Bergman declares the season has been good for Loco Fields. "Things are growing nicely. The beets look wonderful," says Bergman, who came from the technology sector as a network engineer but always enjoyed working with his hands. "I like physical work and like being outside." Seven years ago, he had a change of heart and decided to try something different – and outside. He and his partner, Mindy Griffiths, had been living on some organic farmland and were gardening: it seemed logical to take the next step. "We thought, why don't we try to grow some stuff and bring it to the market?" Things indeed grew, and soon they needed more land: they now work seven acres, 35,000 sq.-ft. of which is unheated tunnel and one small greenhouse. A combination of research, attending agricultural seminars, asking questions, and trial and error was their foundation. "You try something and see what happens," he says. The Loco Fields name was generated out of linguistic playfulness that blends the idea of local with the craziness that can define farming. "Mindy came up with that when we first started. We were just playing around, and it stuck." They grow the usual mixed vegetables, along with dozens of varieties of heirloom tomatoes, much of which heads to the restaurant industry. "We try to keep things new and interesting, including a lot of ginger and turmeric which we sell as a young product," Bergman says. "Before it matures, ginger is bright pink, yellow, and white. It almost has a radish-like texture." Loco Fields is also building up its seed stock of an Andean tuber called oca. "We experiment in the greenhouse and try to grow things that aren't normally grown here."

They sell at area markets, Gentle Rain, and Little Green Grocery, as well as restaurants between Bayfield, London, Kitchener, and Stratford. "For a city of this size, it's crazy how many places there are to go and eat in Stratford. It's quality food, too," Bergman says. He adds that the school has played a significant role in the "constantly changing" dining scene in Perth County. "A lot of the students come out of the chef school and end up in local restaurants. Aaron Linley's door was one of the first I knocked on." He says that chefs are always looking for something new, though when he started, he thought he would visit restaurants and ask them what they wanted. "But I've found they let us do what we're good at. Generally, you get used to what they like just by delivering it and seeing how excited they are. You have that conversation every week." Yet, trying to tailor crops to specific needs is difficult. "To grow and produce exactly that vegetable at that time can be difficult. We're at the whim of the weather and other factors like insects." As for farm-to-table, he describes a scenario in which he's picked vegetables at three o'clock and made the delivery 30 minutes later. "It's then going on a plate at five or six o'clock."

LOCO FIELDS VEGETABLE SOUP FROM A PERTH COUNTY WINTER FIELD

INGREDIENTS

SOUP BASE

1/4 cup	butter
1 lb (454g)	onion, sliced
2 lbs (907g)	Jerusalem artichokes, peeled and diced
1 L (about 4 cups)	chicken stock
	kosher salt

POTATO PURÉE

	kosher salt
1 lb (454g)	fingerling potatoes
1/4 lb (113g)	butter, melted
1/2 cup	whole milk (3%), warmed
1 tsp	squid ink

VEGETABLE GARNISH

500 ml (2 cups)	whole milk (3%)
	garlic clove
	bunch of thyme
2	parsnips, peeled, cut into batons
1	celery root, peeled, cut into batons
2	small turnips, peeled, cut into batons
2	heirloom carrots (different colours if possible), peeled (optional), cut into batons

METHOD

SOUP BASE

In a large saucepan melt butter over medium-low heat. Add onion and sweat, stirring frequently, until very soft and translucent but have taken on no colour (about 10 to 12 minutes). Add Jerusalem artichokes, chicken stock, and simmer until artichokes are tender.

Purée the contents of the saucepan in a blender, pass through a fine meshed sieve, season with salt and reserve until needed.

POTATO PURÉE

In a large saucepan of salted water simmer potatoes until tender. Drain potatoes, then pass them through a ricer, while they are still warm, into a clean saucepan. Fold in the butter and milk, then the squid ink. Season as required and keep warm.

VEGETABLE GARNISH

In a shallow saucepan, combine milk, garlic, thyme, bring to a gentle simmer and gently poach the vegetable batons, over medium to low heat, until they are just tender. Remove from the heat and reserve.

TO FINISH THE DISH

In a deep soup bowl, make a small mound of squid ink-potato puree in the centre. Arrange some cooked vegetable batons on the potato mound and then pour in hot Jerusalem artichoke soup to just cover the vegetables. Serve immediately.

DOWNIE STREET BAKEHOUSE

Alan Mailloux

After a decade in the offices at General Motors, Windsor native Alan Mailloux wanted to create something. "I found my way here because of the Stratford Chefs School. I wanted to be able to use my hands," Mailloux says. Cooking was the answer. He responded to an ad for the school he saw in the Windsor paper – "they were new and casting a wide net for students" – and he and his wife Barb arrived in Stratford in 1990. He graduated in 1992 and cooked in Stratford, St. Marys, and Toronto with Jean-Pierre Challet. Back in Stratford, they opened a bed-and-breakfast and started baking bread for the farmers' market. "That took on a life of its own," he says. "The school taught me the basics, but working in bakeries taught bread production. Two or three loaves of bread compared to 25 loaves is a different mindset." Downie Street Bakehouse opened in August, 2011, and Mailloux has embraced the tactile nature of dough and baking; the corollary is that the shop gets busier each year. "What we bake is very old-fashioned. Flour, water, salt, and sometimes yeast. We make a lot of sourdoughs and ferment them overnight in the fridge, giving them as much time as we can." Slowing the process down is key – the longer it takes to make, the more nutritious it is and the better it tastes, he says. Mailloux's bread is sold at markets in Stratford, London, and Woodstock, and he supplies a few Stratford restaurants. "Many chefs are Stratford grads," he says. "They bake their own breads."

Ten years at General Motors taught Mailloux that he had a single opportunity to know what kind of a job he was doing at his annual performance review. "Cooking is crack cocaine," he says. "I know before anyone else does whether or not what's in front of me is any good. Before the customer knows, before the boss knows. That's an unbelievable rush. In many ways I miss that about the restaurant business." But baking bread is similar, he points out. "When the dough is coming along and has the right feel and right rise and goes in and comes out of the fridge the way we want it to and into the oven, we know along the way." He says an ideal farm-to-table scenario – a luxury in a very small corner of the baking world – is going to farmers and asking them to grow a particular wheat. "I'd commit to buying it all, getting it milled, and making bread with it. But as a small business that's difficult," Mailloux says, conceding that processing and mass production are necessary to feed billions of people. "But there's an awful lot to be said about food that comes from nearby. It's our environment," he says, drawing an analogy. "Planting basil near tomatoes helps keep the bugs away, and they go really nicely together in a sauce. And here we are in this space in Perth County with all this great food around us. It's a similar symbiotic relationship."

NEUBRAND COUNTRY PRODUCE

Laurie Neubrand

It's an unconventional way to sell fresh fruits and vegetables, but Neubrand Country Produce got started in part hawking veggies at Woodland Lake RV Resort in Bornholm northwest of Stratford. "We were growing some produce and I'd do some baking and just drive around the campgrounds Saturday morning. Everybody would be standing there with their wallets," according to co-owner Laurie Neubrand. Located between Mitchell and Monkton, Neubrand's farm is 100 acres, 24 of which and four greenhouses produce food for Perth County. "From asparagus to zucchini," says Neubrand. "We sell a lot of black currants, and we're known for our mesclun." In winter, Neubrand grows in the greenhouses, even though they're not heated: row covers and double-walled construction allow the produce to thrive, without much warmth, amid blustery Perth County snow. Neubrand sells to area businesses – Mercer Hall, The Little Green Grocery, and cafes in the area – and especially at the Stratford Farmers' Market each week. It's been a popular venue for Neubrand's goods for 14 years. "We love our regulars, but we love seeing new customers too. They're always asking what's coming next, and if we don't have certain produce, we'll source it" – something she does by visiting the Elmira Produce Auction Cooperative and a co-op near Lucknow. "I hadn't intended it, but I was at the Bruce-Huron Produce Auction just now and they have more cauliflower ready than we do here, so I have a bin of it in the truck right now." When it's ready to harvest, Neubrand's garlic will

be going into a Provolone focaccia that Downie Street Bakehouse will be making. Other area food purveyors work with Neubrand too. "Ryan [O'Donnell] at Mercer Hall will order a bushel of peas. His staff will have to shell them, so I'm not sure how much they like that," Neubrand says with a smile. "But I'm glad some of our produce goes into the restaurants, and when our customers see our name it's a good feeling. I know they are getting good quality and fresh."

The seemingly innocuous concept of local food has assumed a more freighted and perhaps even dark economic tone of late, given U.S. trade policy. In the past, she has sourced American vegetables in winter but has a hunch that is going to change; call it the realpolitik of produce. "People are starting to say that they don't want to buy American," she says. Yet, the essential life forces of nature trump tariffs. Even though she's witnessed the process for decades, growing the food we eat gives her pause for thought when she observes the relentless insistence of plants to find a way to grow. It happens, she says, when you haven't intended it. "We have black cap raspberries already. They're not field berries, but we've got some canes coming up in the greenhouse. They're ripening fast and we're selling them already." In another greenhouse, a bird dropped, shall we say, a saskatoon seed and a bush grew. "We just left it, and this is the first year we've picked some saskatoon berries off of it."

ROASTED GARLIC AND PROVOLONE CHEESE FOCACCIA

YIELD: ONE 9-BY-13 INCH (23-BY-33 CM) BAKING SHEET

INGREDIENTS

2 lbs (907g)	unbleached, all-purpose flour
26 oz (737 g)	cold water
1 Tbsp	salt
1 Tbsp	instant yeast
4	heads garlic, peeled (the larger the cloves, the better)
1 oz (28 g)	extra-virgin olive oil
4 oz (113 g)	extra-virgin olive oil
8 oz (227 g)	provolone (or Cheddar) cheese, grated

METHOD

Place flour in a large mixing bowl, pour in all but 2 oz (57 g) of the water. Mix to combine with your hands until there is no dry flour left. Scrape any dough off your hands and into the bowl. This will be a very wet dough. Cover bowl with a towel and let it sit for 15 minutes. Sprinkle the salt and then the yeast over the dough and mix to combine with your hands (the salt and yeast need to be evenly distributed). Remove excess dough from your hands, and cover bowl for another 20 minutes.

Stretch and fold the dough by wetting your hands and lifting the edge of the dough from the far end of the bowl up and fold it down towards you. Then lift the edge of the dough closest to you up in the bowl and fold it down away from you over the first fold. Give the bowl a one-quarter turn and repeat the two stretch and folds. Cover the bowl and let dough rest 20 more minutes. Repeat the folding and resting process twice more for a total of three, taking about an hour to complete. When the folding is done, cover the bowl loosely with plastic wrap and refrigerate overnight (12-18 hours). Make sure that the bowl is large enough to accommodate the dough rising a little bit.

Preheat oven to 350F (180 C).

Toss the garlic cloves with the 1 oz (28 g) extra virgin olive oil and place in a small, covered pan (or wrap loosely in aluminum foil). Bake, shaking the pan every ten minutes, until the garlic is soft and lightly coloured (be careful not to burn it). This will take up to 30 minutes.

Remove dough from the fridge. It should be strong but relaxed. Oil your 9-by-13-inch (23-by-33-cm) baking sheet with 2 oz (57 g) of the remaining extra virgin olive oil (this will help prevent sticking). Gently scrape the dough into the oiled pan. Spread the remaining 2 ounces (57 g) oil (or more, if you like) over the dough and use your fingertips to spread the dough out to the four corners of the baking sheet. Cover loosely with a towel and let rise until almost doubled (this could take up to an hour).

Pre-heat the oven to 400F (200C).

Push the cloves of roasted garlic into the dough, distributing evenly. Sprinkle the grated cheese over the dough and bake in the oven until the dough is baked and the cheese is golden brown (about 30 to 40 minutes). If the cheese starts to get a little too dark, cover the pan loosely with aluminum foil until the focaccia is baked.

BENTLEY'S | BAR | INN | RESTAURANT

Breen Bentley

A Stratford native from the other side of the tracks, Breen Bentley is blunt in describing his relationship to the Stratford Chefs School. "I went to the school wanting to make money. I didn't love lamb. I was here to be a capitalist," he says at the same time he's answering patrons' questions at the busy Bentley's reception desk. But he softens the comment adding that the tavern and inn's 6,000 sq.-ft. of space with nearly 60 employees is also inclusive. "We take care of the healthiest and happiest person on one side of the bar and the poorest and the weakest on the other," Bentley says. "I want to take care of everyone." He says the original concept of the school, from which he graduated in 1985, was inspired and made economic sense that helped him achieve his goals. "It was an idea that kept people busy in the quiet times and educated them in the industry." He learned gastronomy, food science, wine pairing, the nuts and bolts of restaurant accounting and business as well as the beauty of food, travel, and life, he says. "The school taught me about the industry and what goals I wanted to set. It was a big piece of the puzzle for me."

In the same breath in which he acknowledges the importance of the Stratford Festival, Bentley insists that tourism is "a surplus" — Bentley's restaurant is for Stratford first. "We're like a train station," he says of its casual nature. "You come

and you sit a bit waiting for somebody. You have a drink and you head out." Quirky architecture means that there're two front doors and one back door at Bentley's and, with 600 customers a day, staff don't greet anyone, just like at a train station. "People just walk in and go where they want to go," he says, adding that he likes it that way. The food is home-made as much as possible, from bread to sauces, but they rely on what he calls "pre-fab." According to Bentley, they serve a lot of onion rings and a lot of alcohol. "I don't stand in great stature when it comes to farm-to-table," he admits. "We're high volume with big trucks [making deliveries]. Someone from Goderich might come with some Lake Huron perch for sale, and while I'd love to be able to write that on the blackboard, it wouldn't be enough for a day's worth of chowder." That reality aside, he says it's freshness, quality, and consistency that are the kitchen's goals for its comfort food. "When you have a bowl of soup or a dessert, it's made here." As for the cooks, not many have come from the school; he's straightforward about that too. "It's hard for me to bring someone like that here." Meanwhile, the clamour of questions, the clatter in the bar area, and the people in constant motion at Bentley's is theatrical. In fact, Bentley is on his stage. "This is my show. It's challenging but I enjoy the show because it's people, drinks, and food. And thank God it makes money too."

BLACK SWAN BREWING CO.

Ryan Stokes

Forager and brewer at Black Swan Brewing Phil Phillips recently added toasted dandelion, burdock, and thistle roots to the downtown Stratford brewery's Road Trip golden ale. "I call it lawnmower beer," Phillips says, stating that the lightly carbonated, fermented beverage is in many ways like a plate of food. "It has flavours that work together and so does beer." He regularly uses foraged wild ingredients in special cask creations, including milkweed, elderflower, and oxeye daisy. "There are a lot of plants that have interesting flavours but have a texture that you wouldn't otherwise want to eat. Bitter ingredients also work well in beer when they wouldn't as food on your plate." That inventiveness, in part, defines Black Swan, according to brewery co-owner Ryan Stokes. The business started on a shoestring budget roughly four years ago with the goal "to take care of our community first" – the people and the restaurants and bars. "We didn't open as a brew pub because the focus has always been on the quality of the beer," he says. "We thought our approach was a business that this community would support and decided to give it a go." Black Swan, the concept of which was formed during what Stokes calls the "pre-craft beer boom," has five core beers and employs 10 – and just as the craft beer industry continues to boom and resonate, Stokes says the brewery has plans to expand tank capacity in 2018. "That's going to allow us to play a bit more, but as we grow we're going to stay relatively small and produce a locally consumed product."

It's a collaborative spirit with restaurants that can generate brewing ideas and styles of beer chefs might like to see, Stokes says, adding that he visits the chefs school to discuss the brewing process and his vision of entrepreneurism. "The students will then come to the brewery for a tour and a tasting. We like to get into the nuances of the beer with them because it allows them to start thinking about pairing beer with food and cooking with it." Stokes, who has spent more than half his life in Stratford and was a science teacher at Stratford Central for nine years – the idea for Black Swan likely came about in discussion with co-owner and fellow teacher Bruce Pepper – says he's impressed with what he calls the "approachability" of the food in the area. "There used to be a sense that there was high-end, expensive food that was unapproachable. I think now there are many restaurants producing fantastic food at a price point and in an atmosphere that is approachable for everybody. And people now recognize there are beers that will pair well with any dish. From a beer standpoint, we've seen a huge cultural shift." The variety of food in Stratford complements beer, he says, with Asian influences on restaurant menus and the strong French influence provided by the school. "It's not fusion, but it's different and interesting," Stokes says. "Stratford has a unique scene because of that."

PAN-FRIED PORK SCHNITZEL WITH BLACK SWAN IPA

We love the pork schnitzel from The Butcher and the Baker in Stratford, which can be used here instead of making your own. Our favourite way to serve pork schnitzel is pan-fried, until crisp and golden brown, and garnished with fries, German-style sauerkraut, lemon wedges, and dill pickles. Our suggested beer pairing is Black Swan IPA, which pours a hazy, golden colour with hints of amber and a medium off-white foam.

INGREDIENTS

PORK SCHNITZEL

4	boneless pork cutlets
1/4 cup	all-purpose flour
1 tsp	kosher salt
1/4 tsp	freshly ground black pepper
2	whole eggs beaten with 2 tbsp water
2 cups	bread crumbs
	butter
	dill pickles
	lemon

SAUERKRAUT

3 Tbsp	vegetable oil
2	white onions, sliced thinly
1 cup	bacon, cooked, roughly chopped
1 cup	light beer, or white wine
1 jar (about 4 cups)	sauerkraut, rinsed and drained

METHOD

PORK SCHNITZEL

Cover the pork cutlets with plastic wrap and pound each one, with a meat tenderizer, until it is about 1/2-inch (1.3cm) thick.

Dredge each cutlet in flour, seasoned with salt and pepper, then the egg mixture and finally the bread crumbs, shaking the cutlet to remove any excess after each coating.

In a skillet over medium-heat, melt butter, add breaded cutlets and cook until crisp and golden brown on both sides (about 2 to 3 minutes per side). Serve warm.

SAUERKRAUT

In a large saucepan, warm vegetable oil over medium-high heat. Add onions and sauté until lightly caramelized (about 3 to 5 minutes). Add the bacon, beer (or wine), sauerkraut and simmer until the flavours have combined (about 20 minutes - do not let dry out).

TO FINISH THE DISH

Arrange pork schnitzel, sauerkraut, dill pickles, and your choice of starch as desired. Finish with a squeeze of lemon over the pork schnitzel and enjoy with a pint of Black Swan IPA!

BON VIVANT PERSONAL CHEF SERVICE AND CATERING

Devin Tabor

The success of a dish he made as a kid just may have sealed the deal and determined a culinary path for Listowel native Devin Tabor. "I had only a slight interest in food as a kid, cooking dinners for the family the odd time," Tabor admits. "It wasn't a passion by any means, but I got some satisfaction the first time I made a grilled vegetable Alfredo dish and everyone loved it. I thought that I could do this." Tabor grew up in Huron County with food and foodservice in the family. His father, uncles, and grandfather were butchers, and he worked in restaurants and grocery stores, but it was while running a family-owned pub for the better part of a decade that a deeper interest in food emerged: it struck him that he wanted to know how to best treat ingredients – both in terms of flavour and technique – in order to cook them properly. He applied to the Stratford Chefs School. "It was demanding. I went to the school because I wanted to learn how to do things right. The fine dining element was a learning curve, but I was impressed with the calibre of the instructors and the professionalism." He graduated in 2004, apprenticed at The Church in Stratford, and cooked at the London Hunt and Country Club, the Little Inn of Bayfield, and other venues. In 2008, Tabor opened his own enterprise, Bon Vivant Personal Chef Service and Catering.

School training and restaurant work proved an ideal blend. "The combined experience in different kitchens while at the school and the knowledge of a variety of techniques were invaluable," he says. "Use the best ingredients, season properly, be professional, and have integrity," adding that the best ingredients come from local producers you know and with whom you've built a relationship. "I use Metzger's just about exclusively. And depending on the season I go right to that particular vegetable producer. We're often friends and we talk and often help each other." Though he's 40 minutes or so from Stratford, Tabor says the food landscape – including the restaurants and the relationships between chefs and farmers – has changed dramatically. "The ingredients and foods you can find in local grocery stores just weren't available when I was in school. Many more towns have farmers' markets now, and I think people are coming back to whole foods and have an interest in eating better and trying new things."

At least part of that renaissance, Tabor believes, has to do with the presence in communities of Stratford graduates and the relationships they create. "I want to develop relationships and foster growth in the industry when it comes to people and employees." He says that makes him feel good. "I helped out with the Ontario Works program at one time, and later I bumped into one of the students. He said that I inspired him to work with food. I don't know where he ended up, but the connection is important to me."

BLYTH FARM CHEESE

Paul Van Dorp

American author and broadcast personality Clifton Fadiman wrote that cheese was "milk's leap toward immortality." His cheese having won the title of best cheese in Canada in 2014, Paul Van Dorp, owner of Blyth Farm Cheese, knows just how far milk can reach. Van Dorp and his wife Heleen were farming in Holland when they moved to the rolling hills of Huron County in 2000. "We brought our cheese equipment with us, but it was a while before we got our OMAFRA permits to produce and sell cheese," Van Dorp says. That process began in 2011, and the transition from northwestern Europe to Ontario's west coast was indeed successful: Blyth Farm Cheese won cheese competitions virtually every year. It's an all-in-one process with animals, dairy, and cheesemaking facility in one location, their 150-acre farm. They have about 400 head of sheep and collect about 3,000 litres of certified organic goat's milk per week. Lee Van Dorp tends the farm and Sarah Reid is a cheesemaker. "We use a Gouda recipe, but we adjust it for the milk we use," says Van Dorp, who took a cheese course with Arthur Hill at the University of Guelph. "That's important to being recognized as a cheesemaker in Ontario," he says. In fact, the quality of Ontario cheese has improved significantly over the past decade, he adds – and consumers have taken notice. "People are looking for local food, and Ontario-made cheese is one specific product they're looking for. We've benefitted from that." The heightened interest among turophiles extends to wanting to see how cheese is made, so Blyth has re-built their facility to make the process visible and engaging. "People are very happy to see how it's made."

Part of what he teaches customers is the terrior of cheese. "If your animals consume pasture or forage on rich soil and a variety of clovers and grasses and other legumes, it affects the milk in a very positive way," Van Dorp says. "There are animals that graze on poor land, and you can see that in the milk." While he says some people don't like the "goaty-ness" of goat's cheese, Van Dorp says Blyth products don't have that quality and they're good for people with lactose intolerance. When it come to the professional kitchen, Blyth gets weekly orders from chefs in the area and the GTA. "They really like the Golden Blyth Aged and Blyth's Cumin," he says. "I find the chefs I deal with very knowledgeable about cheese." A collaboration with Blyth's Cowbell Brewing is in the works too. "They have excellent beer, and we started making a few beer cheeses for them. It looks like we've found one that will be very popular." While he may not be striving for immortality, Van Dorp does marvel at the cheesemaking process. "It never ceases to amaze me that it's almost like a miracle how cheese turns out. It is something that is living, and you have to make adjustments every time because the milk is never the same."

FATHER 'N' SON
RAINY AFTERNOON
BLYTH FARM MAC 'N' CHEESE

You can use any of the Blyth Farm cheeses to satisfy your craving for the love and comfort that is the classic mac 'n' cheese. You could try Blyth's Smoked cheese for smokey mac, a spicy mac using Blyth's Jalapeno, velvety Golden Blyth or Blyth's Cumin. In the recipe below, you can skip the roasted garlic and use Blyth's Garlic cheese instead.

INGREDIENTS

6 cloves	garlic
2 1/2 cups	macaroni noodles
85 g (3 oz)	unsalted butter
85 g (3 oz)	flour
4 cups	milk (2%)
1 tsp	kosher salt
1 tsp	fresh ground pepper
1/2 tsp	nutmeg
8 strips	good quality bacon cooked, cooled and diced
1 package	Blyth Farm Nettle cheese, rind removed, grated
1/2 cup	panko crumbs

METHOD

Set oven for 375F (190C).

Roast the garlic cloves for about 20 minutes or until soft. Cut into small pieces and reserve.

Cook the macaroni noodles in a large pot of salted water until al dente. Drain and reserve.

In a large saucepan, melt the butter and slowly stir in the flour. Cook over medium heat for a few minutes then reduce heat and slowly whisk in the milk. (Optional: add the cheese rind in large pieces that can later be removed.) Cook mixture, over medium-low heat, stirring gently, until it is thick enough to coat the back of a spoon. Reduce the heat and whisk in salt, pepper, and nutmeg. Remove the cheese rinds (if you've added them) stir in the roasted garlic, bacon, grated cheese and cook until the cheese is melted. Add the reserved noodles to the sauce and mix to combine. Pour into an oven-safe pan or casserole dish and bake until hot in the centre (test temperature by inserting a knife into the middle). Sprinkle the mac 'n' cheese with the panko and return dish to the oven to bake until golden brown on top.

THE BRUCE HOTEL

Erin Negus

As pastry chef at The Bruce Hotel in Stratford with its "new Canadian" cuisine, Erin Negus recently created a series of desserts called "Notgia" based on childhood foods. "The desserts bring us back to those points in our lives when we had fun surrounded by foods that made us feel really good and at home," Negus says. "I think my time at the Stratford Chefs School allowed me to think about food in that way." The London, Ontario, native hadn't even been thinking about cooking several years ago; in fact, Negus was attending York University for liberal arts before she decided that the program wasn't really for her. She detoured for a year of baking and pastry at George Brown College, but was still uncertain. "I had no experience in a kitchen, so I wasn't sure what to do or where my career was going to go." Then her parents told her about the Stratford Chefs School. "I applied and was accepted. There was only about a month between George Brown and Stratford. It worked out well, and I'm very happy about it," says Negus, who graduated in 2014. Her time in Stratford has allowed her to see a difference between the schools: food in context. "There's a heightened awareness about where food comes from in Stratford," she says. "The gastronomic community here is very close-knit and passionate. People are really connected to the ingredients, and chefs and teachers have good relationships with farmers." In between first and second year, Negus worked at Pazzo Bakery, and after graduation she worked with chef school alumna Lana Tarrant at Appetizingly Yours in Guelph. She's been at The Bruce since March, 2018. "We do a lot of stuff in-house," Negus says. "There's always something exciting."

Her Stratford training and her work in professional kitchens while a student was critical to understanding the industry. Time management and organization, food preparation, plating, and serving was all eye-opening, she says. "I approach and see my work as art and not just food. I want guests to really like it, but I also make food that I really like and that conveys a message that I want to deliver." Having spent time in larger cities, she sees a binary quality to Stratford when it comes to food and dining. "You have this tourist season where everyone gears up for five months and you're always busy, but at the same time there are places that are really geared to locals. All year round we have this stalwart clientele that love us and carry us through the winter. That's a nice feeling." Having gained some experience over the last few years, Negus says she has the ability to see how opportunities can present themselves. "That was shaped by the school. Coming to this smaller, passionate community really opened my eyes to wanting to do bigger things. Because it's small, it really allows people who are dedicated to follow through with ideas that they've had. It's the reason they got into the industry – to create beautiful things and cook delicious food."

THE BRUCE HOTEL BEEKEEPER

Stuart Arkett

Is it an example of "build it and they will come"? For Stuart Arkett, the hives were already built, and then he arrived to take care of them. "My wife and I own and run a century farm just outside of Stratford. I started keeping bees because there were a few hives on the farm, and I thought it would be cool to learn how to do it." Fast forward to today: "I run about 35 hives and would say I'm one step up from a hobbyist," Arkett says. That said, Arkett has been beekeeper and cash-crop farmer for nearly three decades – and he holds a zoology doctorate, which gives him a scientific perspective with which to consider the pressures bees are under. In a unique initiative, he introduced bees to The Bruce Hotel a few years ago, where there are currently five hives. "I wanted to see how bees would thrive in an urban environment," he says. "It has become quite trendy, and a lot of chefs wear it as a badge of honour to have bees in their operation." Arkett and The Bruce had to get a bylaw changed to enable the hotel to have bees in an urban setting before the hives went onto the property in 2015. "There's lots of green space there, and I'm not surprised that the bees have done really well," he says. The space was originally over-seeded with red clover, which produced a very typical lightly coloured and flavoured clover honey, he notes. There are now dozens of different wildflowers and the diversity and complexity of the ecosystem has given The Bruce's honey has its own "terroir" with a colour and flavour that might be associated with honey from the countryside. On occasion, he brings small groups to see the hives and explain urban beekeeping, and he's toyed with the idea of "wiring" the bees. "Stratford is a very wired city. I've set up a live bee-cam feed to my hives at home. We may do some more wiring of bees at The Bruce in future. It might be a chance to get measurements of temperatures and honey production too."

Arkett is steeped in food culture: he's a baker, and had a wood oven designed and a Stratford stonemason build it. "I also designed a device to roast coffee beans with the residual heat." And his Bruce bees are also steeped in Stratford's food culture. "It's unique for a small town to have such a variety of restaurants and great chefs supporting local producers. The first commercial honey I ever sold was to Balzac's, and Diane took it right away. I think chefs across town love locally produced ingredients, as long as you have a consistent supply and quality." That's an issue with bees: "I never know how much honey I'm going to have from year to year," he says. "I might lose hives in the winter and not have enough, so I'm careful about how many new customers I get. I only take on what I can supply."

BEEHIVE

MAKES ABOUT 12 TO 14 SERVINGS

INGREDIENTS

FOR THE HONEY-ROASTED PECANS

1 cup	pecans
1/3 cup	honey

FOR THE HONEY-NUT CRUNCH

454 g (16 oz)	flour
454 g (16 oz)	brown sugar
454 g (16 oz)	oats
2 cup	pecans, chopped
1/4 cup	honey
454 g (16 oz)	butter, cold, cubed into 1/4-inch (0.6 cm) pieces

FOR THE ITALIAN MERINGUE

5 oz (142 g)	egg whites
1/4 tsp	cream of tartar
10 oz (283 g)	sugar
3 oz (85 g)	water

FOR THE HONEY SEMIFREDDO

600 ml (about 2-1/2 cups)	whipping cream (35%)
2 Tbsp	creamed honey
5	egg whites
200 g (7 oz)	sugar
90 g (3 oz)	honey
125 ml (1/2 cup)	water

METHOD

HONEY-ROASTED PECANS

Preheat convection oven to 350F (180C).

Coat the pecans with the honey and spread over a parchment-lined baking sheet. Bake until bubbling and caramelized, about 10 to 15 minutes. Let the nuts cool and chop until coarsely ground. Reserve for incorporation into semifreddo.

HONEY-NUT CRUNCH

Preheat convection oven to 350F (180C).

Place the dry ingredients into the bowl of a stand mixer fitted with the paddle attachment. Add honey and mix to distribute. Add the butter and mix until crumbs form. Transfer to a parchment-lined baking sheet and bake until golden, about 10 to 15 minutes. Once baked, blitz together the honey-nut crunch until fine crumbs.

ITALIAN MERINGUE

Place egg whites and cream of tartar into the bowl of a stand mixer fitted with the whisk attachment. In a saucepan, add the sugar and water and bring solution to 240F (116C). Once the syrup is at 235F (113C), start whipping the egg whites until frothy. Once the sugar solution has reached 240F (116C), slowly and steadily pour hot sugar syrup into the bowl with frothy whites avoiding hitting the whisk with the syrup. Whip this mixture until cool. Once cool, thick and opaque white, put the mixture into a piping bag until ready to use.

HONEY SEMIFREDDO

Whip cream in a stand mixer until soft peaks form. Add 2 Tbsp creamed honey and continue whipping until stiff peaks form. Transfer cream to a new bowl and chill until ready to incorporate into meringue.

Place egg whites in the clean bowl of a stand mixer with the whisk attachment. In a saucepan, heat the sugar, honey and water stirring to dissolve the sugar and honey. Once dissolved, increase heat to a full boil and bring syrup up to 240F (116C). When syrup is at 235F (113C) start whipping whites until frothy. When sugar syrup has reached 240F (116C), slowly and steadily pour hot syrup into the bowl of the stand mixer while running. Avoid hitting the whisk with any hot syrup mixture. Keep machine running on full speed until bowl is cool to the touch.

Fold the chilled whipped cream into egg white mixture and add chopped honey roasted pecans. Put semifreddo into 2.5-by-3-inch (6-by-8cm) dome-shaped molds and freeze until ready to use. .

TO FINISH THE HIVE

Put the honey-nut crunch into the plate underneath where the semifreddo will be placed.

Invert the semifreddo over top of the crunch and release from the mold. Pipe the meringue in concentric circles around the semifreddo coating it entirely. Torch the Hive to colour the outside.

27 MARKETPLACE

Ian Middleton

For Ian Middleton, farm-to-table reaches to his childhood – and even includes a bit of foraging too. He thanks his British parents' immigration to northern Ontario for that. "They came to Canada in the 1960s and were avid gardeners. They couldn't get things like fresh spinach or shallots," says Middleton. He remembers fresh egg deliveries that were made to the family home and adds that his folks were avid amateur cooks. "There was always a Sunday roast, and they even tried to grow artichokes after a visit to France." Sitting on the patio of 27 Marketplace, where he is executive chef, Middleton describes gathering wild rice, cattails, fiddleheads, and crayfish from Lake Superior and picking wild blueberries, ingredients which perhaps establish a sense of place for him: technically, his birth city, Fort William, doesn't exist any longer, since it amalgamated with Port Arthur to form Thunder Bay in 1970.

After attending Carleton and Lakehead universities, Middleton discovered Stratford and the chefs school. "I came here in 1999 and fell in love with it. I liked the curriculum and the intensity and could walk along the river and be at work in five minutes." The stroll along the Avon has helped keep him here. "I feel like I'm in the countryside," he says. "I can see great architecture and see a play. I'm not commuting, so it's a life-work balance. And people appreciate my cooking." During a ten-year period as a SCS instructor, Middleton taught the basic skills of the school's core programming like holding a knife properly, preparing a brunoise, and food costing, as well as practical cookery. Learning to work with speed and precision is critical, he says. "Students are able to go into a kitchen after graduation and execute without supervision if asked to make mayonnaise or a basic dessert." But there's art, too. "Something that I took away as a student, which is something I have taught, is developing a discerning palate and understanding when something tastes good and when it doesn't."

A stagiaire at Fergus Henderson's iconic nose-to-tail London bar and restaurant, St. John, revealed to him that farm-to-table can be second nature, something that was only starting to happen in Stratford. "Especially with Antony John and Soiled Reputation. It was difficult to find other producers then, but each year you could discover more." Currently, Middleton's cooking uses Soiled Reputation and Church Hill Farm. "We get ducks and duck eggs from McIntosh Farms. I'm buying half a cow in two weeks." It's a collaborative process, he says: sometimes cooks ask for certain products and other times the producers come to the back door and ask if the kitchen wants a specific product they've grown. Yet, to his thinking, farm-to-table is subsumed by local – like the cattails and crayfish of Lake Superior. "When you go to a new restaurant, you ask for what is local, not what is farm-to-table. Local is a culinary identity, things that grow in your area. Here, so many people from the school are now running restaurants that there's a mentality to use local producers. You know them and you know their product."

SOILED REPUTATION

Antony John

According to organic farmer Antony John, Ben Shewry's visit to the Stratford Chefs School a few years ago was emblematic of the way the farm-to-table movement can grow, even on the other side of the world. When Shewry, chef at the acclaimed Attica restaurant in Melbourne, Australia, visited Soiled Reputation, John says it was a mutual epiphany. "He'd never seen a farm like ours before," he says. "He asked about some broccoli that had gone to flower, which I didn't think was edible. Shewry grabbed a handful and started eating. He exclaimed that it was delicious. I thought, of course they're good. We just don't know how to use them. Shewry said that his visit to our farm was inspiration for buying and growing three acres of vegetables only for his restaurant."

John and his wife and business partner Tina Vanden Heuvel have operated Soiled Reputation for nearly three decades, making it a Perth County mainstay in the industry. John himself is a wit and raconteur, an idealist who is a realist painter, a bird watcher and an ecologist. It's not what you might expect from your average farmer. A staff of about 16 take care of 80 acres with 25 acres under cultivation for vegetables. "This is as big as we've ever been," John says, adding that it generates roughly the revenue that a much larger cash crop operation would. "But," he quips, "I don't have to buy a combine." Despite the 30 years of experience, the complexity of the process never fails to humble him. "Sometimes, it feels like a Cirque de Soleil clown wagon. At any moment, one of the wheels could fall off."

The farm's relationship with restaurants started off slowly with the Stratford Chefs School, The Prune, and Rundles, but John and Vanden Heuvel estimated that there was a larger niche. "I wondered if we could provide herbs and vegetables year-round, so I bought a 50-foot greenhouse." By the late-1980s, school graduates would work at a wide range of restaurants and act as ambassadors for John's products. "They got us a lot of winter business in Toronto and Niagara." His experience has also told him that he'd like to see the ratio of meat to vegetables on a plate inverted – something John, who is not a vegetarian, says remains one of the most challenging aspects of his business. Perhaps to that end, Soiled Reputation has recently added yet another product, quinoa, to their repertoire, and are one of only a couple of growers in the province.

Working on what he describes as a terroir concept, he says, "nothing expresses the uniqueness of a region's geography and climate better than the vegetables that come out of its soil. They are a direct distillation, a product of that immediate location." Asked if he's optimistic that the shift to more veg and less meat can in fact happen, John says he wants to see more chefs who have gone through training like that in Stratford. "I hope more people will really see this farm-to-table philosophy and run with it. That's the best you can hope for. Organic food is never going to take over the world. It's always going to be a niche, but I hope there's awareness and discussion that attracts motivated people."

SEARED DUCK BREAST WITH WILTED SOILED REPUTATION MUSTARD GREENS

YIELD: FOUR MAIN COURSES

Antony John and I have known each other for almost two decades, and I have been working with his produce since I moved to Stratford. His products are a revelation, intensely flavoured and beautiful to work with. I love his leafy greens in all their variations, and wanted a dish that showcased his mustard greens, which have an incredible mustard/peppery flavour to them; so something bold was called for and duck for me was a natural pairing.

This dish could be described as a Canadian riff on cassoulet. The beans are cooked with maple syrup to give them a baked bean quality, the wild rice adds nuttiness. The mustard greens give the dish a bit of a bite. By using a pressure cooker to cook the beans, there is no need to pre-soak them, while using a pressure cooker to cook the wild rice keeps it much more flavourful. The sauce is a version of a classic French sweet and sour sauce, a gastrique, to which we have added reduced duck stock to give it lushness. An immersion circulator cooks the duck breast perfectly throughout and all it requires to finish it is a quick sear in a very hot pan to give it colour and render some of the fat.

Traditional cooking methods will also be given for those who do not have the specialized equipment mentioned above. It is important that the greens are gently wilted, to just cook them through, so that they are tender but retain their freshness and piquancy.

INGREDIENTS

FOR THE GASTRIQUE

1/2 cup	sugar
1/2 cup (125 ml)	cider vinegar
1/2 cup (125 ml)	reduced duck or dark chicken stock

FOR THE BEANS

1 cup	dried organic beans
3 Tbsp	maple syrup
2 cups (500 ml)	water
	kosher salt

FOR THE WILD RICE

1 cup	Ontario wild rice
3 cups (750 ml)	water
1 tsp	kosher salt

FOR THE DUCK

4	boneless duck breasts
	kosher salt

FOR THE MUSTARD GREENS

8 oz (227 g)	Soiled Reputation mustard greens
1 Tbsp	butter
	pinch kosher salt

METHOD

FOR THE GASTRIQUE

In a heavy bottomed saucepan pour in the sugar and cook over moderate heat until it is caramelized. Resist the temptation to stir the sugar or you could crystallize it; instead, gently swirl the saucepan to insure an even cooking of the caramel. Once the caramel has been achieved, carefully add the vinegar all at once, it will splutter so caution is required. The sugar at this point will clump together, using a whisk stir to dissolve the sugar into the vinegar, then add the stock. You may need to reduce the gastrique a bit (until it is thick enough to coat the back of a spoon). Reserve.

FOR THE BEANS

If using a pressure cooker, place one tablespoon of maple syrup, the beans and the water into the pressure cooker, cook on high for 20 minutes then use the quick release to vent the pot. Drain the beans, drizzle on the remaining maple syrup, season with a little salt and reserve.

For the traditional method, soak the beans overnight, drain and place them in 6 cups (1500 ml) of fresh water. Boil until tender, about one hour, then drain, drizzle with maple syrup, season with salt and reserve.

FOR THE WILD RICE

Place all the ingredients into the pressure cooker and cook on high pressure for 13 minutes. Vent using the quick release method.

For the traditional method add rice and 6 cups of water (1500 ml) to a saucepan. Bring to a boil and simmer for about 45 minutes, until the grains have become tender. Drain, season and reserve.

FOR THE DUCK

Set the immersion circulator's temperature to 136F (58C) and use it to warm a container full of water, that is large enough to hold the duck breasts, to the desired temperature. Season the duck breasts with kosher salt then place them in a re-sealable plastic bag and lower into a water bath to push the air out of the bag (or use a vacuum sealer) and then seal. Put the bag in the heated water and cook the duck for a minimum of one hour, up to four. Just before serving, remove the duck from the bag, pat dry, heat a heavy bottomed skillet, that can hold all of the duck breasts without crowding them, over medium heat. Sear the skin side of the duck breasts until some of the fat has rendered and the skin has turned deep mahogany colour.

For the traditional method, pre-heat an oven to 450F (230C). Season the duck breasts with salt. Place a large heavy bottomed skillet over medium heat, place the duck breasts in the skillet skin side down, and then place into the pre-heated oven. Cook until the internal temperature of the duck reaches 130F (54C) (about 10-12 minutes depending on your oven). Let the duck breasts rest for 5 minutes (the internal temperature will continue to rise).

FOR THE MUSTARD GREENS

In a large sauté pan, add a tablespoon of butter, the mustard greens and pinch of salt. Sauté until just wilted.

TO FINISH THE DISH

Add the beans and rice to the slightly wilted greens and warm through. Place a tidy mound of the greens mixture onto the centre of a plate. Carve the duck breast into thin slices and place over top of the greens mixture. Drizzle the gastrique around and over the duck. Serve immediately.

REVEL

Jordan Lassaline

They called them "bread hands," and Stratford Chefs School alumnus Jordan Lassaline and his classmates were amazed by them. It was iconic Montreal baker James MacGuire's visits to the School that made an impact on – and indirectly set a goal for – the revel executive chef. A Petrolia, Ontario, native, Lassaline graduated in 2005 and cooked at the Prune and Bijou, and as well in Toronto with Jamie Kennedy, where he was a baker. Years later, he finds himself very much at home in Stratford and with that most elemental foodstuff, bread.

"Making bread is a skill I've really enjoyed honing. It didn't come easily or quickly, but you saw incremental change over years. We watched MacGuire work at the school, and he made it look so simple. Then you'd touch the dough, and it would immediately stick to your hands and tear. I don't have bread hands like his, but they are definitely better than they were," Lassaline says with a laugh. He describes how over time his breads began to improve: the crust became more shiny; the crumb lighter; the air pockets more random. While he cooked in fine dining and has been an instructor at the School, now at revel, and with a focus on baking, he's discovered where his true culinary focus is. "Revel owner Anne Campion and I share a commitment to certain products and quality. We have high expectations of our final products." It's a similar commitment he finds in the Stratford community with colleagues, restaurants,

and producers supporting each other. "That's something I never really found in Toronto. There wasn't that personal connection you get here," he says. "Here, producers have a vested interest in your success because it means you'll continue to do business with them and vice versa." Lassaline adds that the school brings Stratford an influx of talent and people interested in restaurants and cooking farm-to-table, and they bring fresh ideas and ambitions for the kitchen. At the same time, he cautions that farm-to-table isn't a label or highlighting a few farm names on a menu. "It has to be a relationship and include conversation with producers about their farming practices. They come into your restaurant or café, or send their friends, so you have this network of people supporting local food and the local economy."

Best practices and the bread hands example, in a way, are at the core of Lassaline's philosophy; watching proper techniques demonstrated at the school were touchstones he relies on today. "Do things the best way," he says. "There are shortcuts that make it easier than doing things from scratch the proper way. What we do at revel are simple products, but we're making everything from high quality ingredients and not cutting corners to make a job 15 minutes shorter. Taking those extra steps and doing things precisely and, in a way, traditionally, really comes out in the end as a lot more special, even when it's something as simple as a breakfast bun."

TNT BERRIES

Nadia Walch

Drive the long, gently sloping gravel laneway adjacent to a field of nondescript bushes and you'll be passing sea buckthorn berries at TNT Berries in Shakespeare. The deciduous shrub's bright yellow or orangey egg-shaped berry is a fruit thats full culinary possibilities haven't yet nearly been met, according to producer Nadia Walch. "They're tart and people don't gravitate to tart things," she says. Blueberries, however, are a different matter. "Everybody knows blueberries and loves them."

The family started growing them in Haysville in 2001, initially on a single acre, so the kids had something to do in the summers – Tillo, Natasha, and Toby lent their first names to the eponymous "TNT Berries" business. It's grown to much more: they bought the current 110-acre property in 2007 and, laboriously, moved hundreds and hundreds of blueberry bushes. And each year, it's a lot of preparatory work leading up to three to four weeks of a late-summer harvest that will yield four to five kilograms per bush. The last few years, blueberry sales to Stratford restaurants – but to a lesser degree sea buckthorn berries – have grown significantly, says Walch. "There's a great variety of foods in Stratford, and the chefs are amazing. It's an extra attraction for people. They're not just coming for the theatre; they know they're going to get good food."

She estimates that restaurant purchases account for up to 30 percent of their sales: word-of-mouth in a tightly-knit agricultural community has been responsible. "It's easy for me. Chefs call and say they need berries," says Walch. Bijou, Revel, and Mercer Hall, with chef-graduates of the Stratford Chefs School, visit TNT and buy berries from the farm's walk-in freezer. Many chefs haven't seen a blueberry bush. "A lot of them don't know how they grow," Walch says. "But once they pick them, they are more willing to pay the price because they realize how challenging and labour-intensive it is." Walch admits that sea buckthorn has a distance yet to go to find a spot at table. TNT has 150 plants, which tolerate salty soil well and are wind-pollinated, requiring no bees. The family doesn't spray their berries and uses netting against birds. "They may eat some berries, but they also help control other pests. We are environmentally friendly, though that cuts into your profits," says Walch, pointing out that people love to talk about organic and natural but are often reluctant to pay for it. "The words are easy but don't always represent the work done on the farm. Many people don't have a concept of what goes into getting it to the table." She acknowledges, though, that the stories about where food comes from are part of a city's restaurant culture, and enjoys knowing a chef is using TNT berries. "It makes you feel good. You think, I had a part in this. There's pride that goes with that knowledge."

Walch pauses as she explains. Just outside the kitchen window, a woodpecker and goldfinch share some time together skittishly at the bird feeders. A hundred metres beyond, TNT blueberry and sea buckthorn bushes along the laneway, still quiet in the cool of May, await the heat of the summer months.

TNT BLUEBERRY BUNS

Yield: About 30 buns

INGREDIENTS

FOR THE FILLING

675 g (24 oz)	blueberries, fresh or frozen
1 1/2 lbs	butter
720 g (25 oz)	raw sugar
2 1/4 Tbsp	ground cardamom
10 g (0.4 oz)	kosher salt
1 1/4 cups	Vanilla Pastry Cream (recipe follows)

FOR THE DOUGH

1 recipe Yeasted Bun Dough
(recipe follows)

FOR THE CITRUS SYRUP

1 cup (250 ml)	water
1 cup	raw sugar
2	oranges
3	lemons

TO FINISH THE DISH

Cream Cheese Icing (recipe follows)

METHOD

Place the blueberries in a saucepan with a splash of water and bring to a simmer, over medium heat, stirring often to avoid scorching.

Allow the berries to simmer for a few minutes until they burst and release their juices. Strain the berries from the juice, reserving both the juice and the berries.

Set the berries aside to be used later when assembling the buns. Return the juices to the saucepan and reduce until 3/4 of a cup, or less, remains and juices are thickened. Chill the berries and juice completely.

Beat the butter and raw sugar in a stand mixer, using the paddle attachment, until light and fluffy. Add the cardamom and salt, and mix to combine.

Scrape the bowl down and, with the mixer running, drizzle in the reduced blueberry juice. Scrape again and beat until well blended. Set the blueberry butter aside at room temperature.

Roll the bun dough into a long sheet, about 16-inches (40 cm) wide and about a 1/3-inch (0.7 cm) thick.

Spread the blueberry butter evenly over the dough, leaving a border at the top and bottom. Spread the Vanilla Pastry Cream over top of the blueberry butter and finally scatter the cooked berries over the half of the Vanilla Pastry Cream closest to you.

Roll the dough up snugly, jelly roll style.

Use a knife to cut the dough into 160 gram (6 oz) buns (about 30 buns). Arrange buns in greased 9-by-13-inch (23-by-33 cm) dish, about a dozen buns to each dish. At revel we place them into individual greased 4-inch wide stainless steel ring moulds placed on lined baking sheets. In either case, wrap the pans loosely with plastic wrap or cover the buns with a clean, damp towel to prevent them from drying out while they rise.

Allow the buns to rise at room temperature for an hour.

As the buns rise, preheat your oven to 425F (220C) (still oven, not convection).

To check if they are ready to bake, uncover them and poke one gently with your finger. If the dough springs back quickly, cover them again and let them sit for a further 20 minutes and check again. The buns are ready to bake when they slowly spring back leaving a slight impression where they were pressed (rising time will depend on the temperature of your dough and the room).

Bake the buns in the preheated oven for 5 minutes and then reduce the temperature to 375F (190C). Bake for a further 25 minutes. Check that the buns are done by pressing on the centres. If the centre springs back and the buns are nicely golden, they are done. Buns baked in a 9-by-13-inch (22-by-33 cm) dish may take up to an additional 10 minutes to finish.

While the buns bake, make the Citrus Syrup by combining the water and sugar in a small saucepan. Zest one of the lemons and one of the oranges into the mixture. Then squeeze a half cup of juice from the oranges and a half cup of juice from the lemons into the saucepan.

When your buns are baked, allow them to cool for 10 minutes, or until they are still warm but safe to handle, before removing them from the pan or ring moulds. Heat the Citrus Syrup to a boil and then drizzle evenly over the buns, using the entire amount of syrup. Leave the buns to cool and soak up the Citrus Syrup before garnishing with the Cream Cheese Icing.

YEASTED BUN DOUGH

INGREDIENTS

560 g (20 oz)	stirling whey butter
2060 g (72 oz)	organic hard flour
41 g (1.5 oz)	kosher salt
250 g (9 oz)	organic raw sugar
750 g (27 oz)	whole milk (3%)
470 (17 oz)	free run eggs
35 g (1.2 oz)	instant dry yeast

METHOD

Melt the butter and then set it aside to cool until just warm.

Combine the flour and salt in a mixing bowl and stir to combine.

Combine the sugar, milk and eggs in the bowl of the mixer and whisk them together. Sprinkle the yeast over the surface. Allow the yeast to soften for a few minutes.

Whisk the yeast into the liquid ingredients before adding the flour mixture and the melted, cooled butter.

Mix on first speed, using the dough hook. After the dough comes together, check the consistency and moisture and adjust with more flour or liquid, if necessary. The dough should be soft and slightly sticky.

Mix the dough for 10 minutes, total, on first speed.

Transfer to a storage container and refrigerate overnight.

The next day, lightly flour and roll the dough out into a long rectangle about 1/2-inch (1.3 cm) thick. Fold in thirds (as you would a letter) transfer to a baking sheet, wrap in plastic wrap and let the dough rest, refrigerated, for an hour to relax before rolling and shaping buns.

CREAM CHEESE ICING

INGREDIENTS

1 cup	butter, softened
2 cups	icing sugar
2 cups	cream cheese, softened to room temperature
1 tsp	vanilla extract
1/2 tsp	salt

METHOD

Place the butter in the bowl of a stand mixer fitted with the paddle attachment.

Whip butter until it is light and fluffy. Add the icing sugar in several stages while mixing on low speed. Once the icing sugar is incorporated, increase the speed and mix until butter-sugar mixture is smooth and light. Scrape the bowl well and beat again to ensure the mixture is free of lumps.

Beat in the cream cheese, vanilla and salt. Scrape the bowl and beat again.

Store the icing in the fridge but bring to room temperature before using.

VANILLA PASTRY CREAM

INGREDIENTS

2 cups (500 ml)	whole milk (3%)
1/2	vanilla bean, seeds scraped
240 g (9 oz)	sugar
66 g (2 oz)	flour
1/2 tsp	kosher salt
6	egg yolks
2 Tbsp	butter

METHOD

Place the milk in a medium sauce pan, reserving about 1/2 cup (125 ml). Split and scrape the vanilla bean and add both the pod and seeds to the milk. Heat the milk until steaming without allowing the milk to boil, then set aside to infuse.

Meanwhile, combine the sugar, flour, and salt in a large mixing bowl and whisk to combine and break up any lumps.

Add the egg yolks and the reserved cold milk to the flour mixture and whisk until smooth.

Slowly temper the hot milk into the egg yolk mixture while whisking constantly. Return the entire mixture to the saucepan.

Heat the mixture gently, while stirring constantly with a spatula, until the mixture simmers and thickens. Whisk the mixture for a minute or two while it simmers to ensure it is fully thickened.

Pass the pastry cream through a fine-meshed strainer and whisk the butter into the hot mixture.

Transfer to a storage container and press a layer of plastic wrap directly onto the surface of the cream. Refrigerate until cold before putting a lid on the container.

BLACK DOG VILLAGE PUB AND BISTRO

Kathleen Sloan-McIntosh

Restaurateur and author Kathleen Sloan-McIntosh has owned Black Dog Village Pub and Bistro in Bayfield for 13 years. She, along with co-owner and husband Ted McIntosh, is friend to the Stratford Chefs School: she's written about it and she has a graduate, Nathaniel Beattie, as an executive chef. About 50 minutes west of downtown Stratford, the restaurant's shaded patio, near the east shore of Lake Huron, is still cool at 10 a.m. as she discusses the school's role in the industry across Canada using words like integrity, passion, currency. "When you're linked with someone from the school, you know they're serious about being a chef and that they've learned the skills from someone who knows what they're doing." She speaks in quiet tones that contrast with the sharp ringing sounds of construction that fill the empty streets and, along with a slowly building mid-morning heat, anticipate the busy season. Beattie and the Black Dog kitchen will serve over 400 customers on a summer Saturday.

Toronto-born, Sloan-McIntosh moved to England to work in marketing and advertising when she was 18. When she returned to Canada, she wrote for newspapers and magazines and has since published several food and cook books, including A Year in Niagara: The People and Food of Wine Country and Simply the Best: Food and Wine from Ontario's Finest Inns, to name only a few. After four years in Niagara, she returned to Toronto – and realized she enjoyed being outside big cities. "Researching Ontario inns, we were visiting Bayfield and learned that The Admiral was for sale. We saw what it could be." They bought the building, renaming it Black Dog. "Then, the concept of farm-to-table was a work-in-progress, and I was amazed that I couldn't find local products. That's changed in the last five years, and we now have a Bayfield Market that is served by local farms, but it wasn't like that before." Citing Niagara's Stephen Treadwell as a pioneer who collaborated with farmers to get the produce he wanted, she points to Antony John as a Perth County example. "Toronto chefs were soon buying from Soiled Reputation." The school, she says, has nurtured that chef-producer relationship. "You now have a generation of young chefs for whom farm-to-table is not a new phenomenon. It's just the way it should be."

But there is a new phenomenon against which she says the school is a bastion: the young cook as over-reaching pop culture celebrity, fuelled partly, at least, by the food media. According to Sloan-McIntosh, when the school interviews prospective students hoping to attend and asks why they want to be a chef, the answer required is simple and straightforward: "'I love cooking, and I can't imagine doing anything else.' The school has had that kind of impact," she says. It's why she hopes for more connections between SCS and restaurants like Black Dog in the future. "I have a lot of respect for the school and the students and the way they do things."

METZGER'S MEAT PRODUCTS INC.

Gerhard Metzger

If one aspect of the food industry has changed dramatically over the decades, it is likely that of butchery and the meat counter. In many places in the province, a few old-school butchers keep the tradition alive – and are helping it grow – in the face of grocery store meat departments carrying proteins that are processed at central plants and packed into Styrofoam trays for display on the shelves. Gerhard Metzger represents one of those butchers. He started his business, Metzger's Meat Products, in 1990 in Hensall, Ontario, about 40 minutes west of Stratford. Today he employs 17 people, and his products reach across Ontario. "It originally was a small country abattoir which basically catered to farmers and farm-gate markets for custom processing," Metzger says. He arrived in Canada from Stuttgart, Germany, when he was 22 years old and bought the facility when he was 24. His wife Heike and their children Jason and Stephanie are part of the business. From the beginning, Metzger's had a retail presence and served the restaurant industry as well. Over time, Gerhard Metzger made it a priority to increase the range of products he made as the abattoir side of the business fell away. "To have live animals on the one side and ready-to-eat foods on the other is difficult," he notes. Metzger's works with local producers and supplies many restaurants with special cuts and products that they make to order for special menu options, and use local farmers and packers to do so. If a restaurant needs a particular product, Metzger's prides itself on being able to work with the chef and come up with a solution. "We can create something that is unique to that customer like a Frenched loin chop which they may not be able to easily source," he says.

After three decades in the business, Metzger has watched as his customers' interest in basic pork chops and hamburgers has shifted to more unique products, flavours, and spices. "We've seen a big change and people are more adventurous and knowledgeable. They're willing to try different things. Ten years ago, we'd make special items and they wouldn't sell." People are looking for good quality and no additives, Metzger says, listing cuts like flat iron steak, which you didn't see 20 years ago, or pork shoulder. "There are better cuts, and it's a matter of how they are cooked. If you prepare it right, you can make a better tasting meal out of a lesser cut. So the demand has changed for some cuts which used to be converted into other things." Metzger's has plans for the next several years to expand their retail presence, though their reach is already quite wide: you might even find their pepperoni sticks at area gas stations. But regardless of where the product is found, Metzger says relationships are what count. "Over the years, customers start to trust you. It's not just about the business of making money. There's reward in having a happy customer too. That's how we grew over the years."

CHAR SIU PORK SHOULDER

When we first opened the Black Dog Village Pub & Bistro in Bayfield in 2005, it was my goal to feature as many quality local food producers on our menu as possible. The first one I approached – since I had heard so many good things about them – was Metzger Meats located in Hensall, only a short drive away.

Gerhard Metzger hails from Germany, so it's no surprise that he features superlative pork products. From the world's best bacon on our Caesar salad to the smoked sausage served with our warm pretzels to pork loin, back ribs, tenderloin, belly and shoulder, we have systemically worked our way through the offerings found at Metzger's for menu staples and specials alike. We're fortunate to have the Metzger family on our doorstep.

This recipe features one of my favourite pork cuts: shoulder. It is unfailingly tender and delicious and, while it takes a bit more effort to achieve this – trimming and slow-cooking – the results are more than rewarding. Char siu is basically Chinese barbecue sauce and, while it is very easy to make, you will also find jarred versions of it available in large supermarkets, specialty food shops, and certainly Asian food markets.

In this preparation, boneless pork shoulder is trimmed of excess fat, cut into chunks, and slow-braised before being treated to this absolutely delicious, sticky, fragrant sauce. As an appetizer you can serve it in lettuce cups, sprinkled with sesame seeds and finely chopped green onion. Or, as a main course with simple steamed rice and baby bok choy or other greens. Make the char siu sauce first and set to one side while you prepare the pork.

INGREDIENTS

FOR THE CHAR SIU

1/2 cup	hoisin sauce
3/4 cup	liquid honey
1/2 cup (125 ml)	soy sauce
1/4 cup (63 ml)	shaoxing (Chinese cooking wine)
2 tsp	Chinese 5-spice powder
2 Tbsp	fresh gingerroot, grated
8 cloves	garlic, finely minced
1/2 tsp	red chili flakes (optional)

FOR THE PORK

4 lb (1.8 kg)	boneless pork shoulder, excess fat trimmed, cut into 2-inch (5 cm) chunks
2 Tbsp	olive oil
1	large onion, sliced
1/2 tsp	salt
1/2 tsp	freshly ground black pepper

TO FINISH THE DISH

Sesame seeds
Finely chopped green onion
Butter lettuce

METHOD

Preheat oven to 350F (180C).

Choose a large, oven-proof baking dish for the pork. Add the pork chunks to the dish along with the olive oil and sliced onion. Add salt and pepper and toss together thoroughly. Use heavy-weight aluminium foil to cover the dish snugly. Place in the preheated oven and bake for 1 hour. After an hour, pull the dish from the oven, remove the foil and add the prepared sauce to the pork. Stir this mixture well into the pork and the liquid that has accumulated: it is important not to drain this liquid.

Return the dish to the oven and continue to bake for another 30 minutes. Then, give the mixture another stir and return to the oven for another 30 minutes. At this point, test a piece of the pork to see if it is done to your liking – it should be tender but not falling apart. If it is as you like it, remove from the oven, sprinkle with sesame seeds and chopped green onion and serve with butter lettuce. If you continue baking, be careful not to over-bake, otherwise the pork will become too dry.

SIRKEL FOODS

Kelly Ballantyne

When she was 24, and had worked in the restaurant industry since she was 14, Kelly Ballantyne decided as a matter of fact that she wanted to go to chef school. "I'd always worked as a server," says Ballantyne, who was born and raised in Stratford. While working front-of-the-house at York Street Kitchen, she was invited to work in the back-of-the-house. "They said I'd be good in the kitchen." She was, and so she went to Stratford Chefs School. After graduating in 2000, and after her apprenticeship at York Street along with positions in other Stratford kitchens, she opened Sirkel Foods in 2005. The arc of her restaurant's growth has been based on a theory of simplicity that she studied at the school. "I learned amazing things from Neil and Bryan [veteran Stratford Chefs School instructors and former Rundles and The Old Prune chefs Baxter and Steele, respectively], and I always start with those fundamentals and building blocks. You don't have to mess with the ingredients too much. Use the most delicious piece of meat with the most delicious sauce. When you eat something, it's sweet, sour, bitter, and salty. It's about simplicity, but simplicity doesn't have to be boring."

It was a relatively short transition from chef-in-training to entrepreneur, and the busy restaurant on Wellington Street has proven itself for over 13 years serving homemade, casual, and fresh food for breakfast and lunch. "We make as much as we can from bread to soups and all of our pastries." The Sirkel kitchen draws on the fundamentals of her formal culinary training, but Ballantyne says, "I like getting things made and tasting delicious quickly." A summer lunch can mean 46 full seats and a lineup on the sidewalk, with the take-away line just about as long. While price – and what she stresses is "good food fast" – has made the restaurant popular, it's community support that helps sustain it. She once posted on social media looking for rhubarb and offered a sandwich as a barter. "We got so much rhubarb, about 10 pails, just from what local people had in their backyards," she says. Similarly, if a producer comes to the back door, Ballantyne will more often than not buy the product. "For me, you just know a fresh tomato is going to taste really good." The kitchen calls Sheldon Berries in Zorra Township anxiously waiting for strawberries, raspberries, and blueberries. It's part and parcel of the food scene in Stratford and Perth County. "It's a rich culture compared to a lot of small cities. We're pretty awesome. There's crazy-fancy and casual. And it's a mix that now includes three vegan restaurants," she says adding that there is restaurant cross-promotion. "What you can't find at one will be at another. Soup Surreal will send us customers who are looking for a sandwich, and we refer to other restaurants." Over time, Ballantyne says that Sirkel Foods has tailored what it does to fit a particular niche in the Stratford restaurant community rather than trying to do everything for everyone. "We're really good at making sandwiches, salads, soups, and pastries, so that's our focus now, and being consistent at it."

C'ESTBON CHEESE LTD.

George Taylor

The original settlers, demobilized soldiers who arrived following the Boer War in the early 1900s, dubbed a tract of land only minutes southwest of St. Marys "Transvaal Farm." Today, it's home to C'estBon Cheese. George Taylor has owned the 200 acres since the 1980s when he started making cheese after retiring from television sports production. "It was a weekend retreat from Toronto, a place to decompress," Taylor says. The farm had been primarily cash crops with Hereford cattle, Suffolk sheep, and Boer goats, but Taylor was looking to produce something unique. "I could have brewed beer, baked bread, or made cheese, all involving fermentation." Taylor choose cheese – and the vehicle for the curds was goat's milk. "Goats are amicable. I was familiar with them from having meat goats here. Mostly though, goats were not under any supply or quota management," he says frankly. The research done, and the recognition that chevre was popular on restaurant menus, Taylor invested in a good quality herd and started the dairy in 1999. "I wanted a small operation, a micro-business, where I could make cheese more or less at my leisure." It became a much more successful business than he expected but, he maintains, "I still can make cheese when I want to make cheese."

When the demand for his flagship chevre outstripped the capacity of his herd to supply the milk, he changed the business model and started sourcing milk from Perth County goat farmers, mostly Amish and mostly within 20 miles of each other. Scaling back on the dairy side of the operation gave him the flexibility he originally wanted. "We have a happy balance here." Focussing on fresh product means less time commitment and no expensive storage for aging: the process of taking the milk and shipping out fresh cheese is a Monday-to-Thursday time-frame. "But I think of the cheese as an artisanal, hands-on, and authentic goat's cheese," he says, referring to himself as something of a "cheese hermit" – the facility is indeed tucked out of the way, and though he is a self-described "one-man operation," he only likes making cheese and not selling it. He admits, though, that he's happy that it does seem to sell well, or the whole enterprise would have ground to a halt long ago.

Good food products and the ingredients that make them are important to the economy and culture of the area as far as Taylor is concerned. Stratford has always been a consistent market for him and sales have grown by word of mouth rather than by active promotion and marketing, he says, adding that chefs like the cheese itself and the convenience of the rigid resealable container. Yet, he senses a change too, and anticipates more local, heritage food being prepared. "Stratford has a good number of fine dining establishments, and the culinary scene is going through a renaissance as the old guard steps aside for the new players who are bringing a new concept of global cuisine and using local products."

SIRKEL
DREAM-WICH

Good ingredients, a range of textures, some spicy heat, and delicious flavours can
make the humble sandwich a "Dream-wich."

INGREDIENTS

2 slices	fresh whole wheat bread
1/2 cup	C'estBon fresh chèvre, warmed at room temperature
2 Tbsp	Rootham Tangy Red Pepper Jelly
	a handful of organic arugula
5	thick slices of oven roasted chicken breast

METHOD

Take the slices of bread and lay them on a cutting board. Spread the chèvre on both slices making sure to cover right to the edges to ensure a perfect bite every time. Spread the jelly on top of the chèvre on both slices. Season the chicken as you prefer and place it on one of the bread slices. Top with the arugula, put the sandwich together, cut and enjoy!

MERCER | KITCHEN | BEER HALL | HOTEL

Ryan O'Donnell

A meal on a Spanish mountainside reinforced for Ryan O'Donnell that food and cooking are communal. "Between the first and second years at Stratford, I staged at Ferrero, near Alicante. We worked and lived together intensely, and one of my most memorable meals was with them up a mountain and cooking snails and rustic dishes on an open fire with jugs of Spanish wine. I'll never forget it." Community continues to resonate for O'Donnell: it kept him in Stratford after graduation. "I had fallen in love with it. And under instructors and cooks like Bryan Steele, I saw the wealth of produce we have, how truly farm-to-table we are. I experienced that in other countries but not as close as here. We have five or six farmers come through the back door every week."

A 2010 Stratford Chefs School graduate, O'Donnell oversees the kitchens at The Prune and Bar 151, Mercer Kitchen and Beer Hall, and York Street Kitchen. After a decade in film production in Toronto, he started cooking and decided Stratford was the best school to get the knowledge he wanted. The practical and theoretical education had a massive impact on him, and when he started teaching at Stratford, he says, "that accelerated my abilities as a chef." As an instructor, he's examined the environment. Much like the mountainside meal, he takes a view from high up to describe farm-to-table: he sees the romantic ideal of a farm supplying a restaurant community but cites a shared obligation to see to its care and evolution. "We need better farming practices, and we need to be responsible and mindful of how and what we as restaurants consume and what it's costing us in terms of the environment and future generations." Collaboration is essential. "There is a lot of discussion, especially in late winter, of what we might be looking for this year, or talk of products or livestock breeds that we haven't offered in the past that we'd like to explore now." If one restaurant wants only shoulders, for instance, suppliers will look for another restaurant in town that is looking for loins. "Between two or three of us, they know they have a market for that product," he says. While a farmer raising a few pigs and with a small vegetable patch can serve part of the restaurant industry – and the public who are willing to pay for it – can it work on a large scale, he asks? "We try to blend the two with organic farmers and farmers doing conventional feed with pastured chicken that is being raised just for us. We also use farmed fish but are very careful about where it is being farmed and buying through companies that we trust are vetting their suppliers."

O'Donnell won't get any argument that Stratford restaurants have flourished because of the great producers around them whose businesses, in turn, have grown because of the restaurants. "It's symbiotic," he says. "Chefs here are trying to push that further."

MCINTOSH FARMS

Erin McIntosh

You'll find farmers on both sides of Erin McIntosh's family. Her husband Shawn's parents are farmers in Mount Forest and her own father runs a commercial pork operation in Hesson, but the fact that McIntosh Farms produces grass-fed and pasture-raised meat and eggs makes for an interesting family dynamic – one that represents two solitudes of animal husbandry. "My father comes here and sees our pigs out on the grass and says, 'Put those pigs inside. They're going to wreck your pasture!'" Erin says. But free-roaming pigs rooting about and snuffling on pasture is entirely the point of McIntosh Farms. The 50 acres in Atwood, Ontario, on the border of Huron County, is home to 25 head of grass-fed cattle, as well as sheep, pigs, and hundreds of ducks and chickens and guinea fowl. "We just love animals," she says. Within that declaration is a soft-spoken and genuine sense of pride in the way they farm and the care with which they do it.

A dynamo who oversees farm operations at the same time she is a mother to four young children under the age of 12, McIntosh describes Perth County as "a hub for food and farmers." The farm switched to a grass-fed program in 2012, and growth was steady. They started at Stratford's Slow Food Market five years ago, and over time, awareness of what they were doing with their livestock drew attention, including that of the students at the school. "I've met many Stratford Chefs School students at the market. They will leave for some time after they've graduated and get some experience in Toronto, but they often come back. I will see them a year or two later, and they will want to use our products." In 2015, when the Stratford Chefs League held a "Call to Farms" at McIntosh Farms, their reputation grew. "That just opened the floodgates," McIntosh says. The metaphor, however, is not one of an uncontrollable force; rather, she smiles at the thought of it. "I find it's really easy. The chefs are straightforward and I'm straightforward, so I really enjoy the relationships." The next step in the relationship is what ends up on the plate. "The chefs take something that we have produced and make something spectacular to eat. They pay it homage."

McIntosh sees the Stratford students' training as allied with social and environmental responsibility. That's a basic tenet at McIntosh Farms. Working with Mercer Hall's Ryan O'Donnell for the recipe in this profile, McIntosh says she shares similar values with him and chefs like him. "They are conscious about where their meat comes from," adding that ecology and animal welfare are paramount. "We're at a tipping point in our food system, and we need to change people's views." Perhaps counter-intuitively, McIntosh has her own call to farms for that: she'd like to see more people eat less meat but eat better meat. "Chefs like Ryan want to use good meat that was raised properly. We need the next generation of chefs to seek out these types of products, too."

MCINTOSH FARMS SMOKED DUCK RICE BOWL

Mercer's duck bowl is one of the most popular dishes we've ever created. So much so that since it went on the menu in the summer of 2016, it hasn't ever left. That is a significant feat considering there are no other dishes in its category that stay on the menu much longer than six months.

The origin of this dish comes partly from the practical necessities of running a high volume kitchen that preps all its 50-plus menu items from scratch as well as a desire to provide one of our favourite local producers a steady outlet for their animals. We wanted to use whole ducks from Erin McIntosh because they were the best value for money in game. This is especially true when all of the parts (bones to breast to livers) fulfilled a need in our menu. From a producer point of view, it was far more efficient for Erin to be selling us whole duck than finding separate outlets for the breasts, legs and carcass. Win, win.

The flavours in this duck rice bowl are vaguely reminiscent of Peking duck: sweet, sticky and smoky. Fresh, herbal flavours are important here as they brighten the dish and keep it from being overly sweet. The real make-or-break factor in the bowl is the skin of the duck being caramelized and golden brown. It adds a tremendous texture and flavour when done to the perfect finish. The addition of a fried duck egg (from the same farm) adds richness and texture while completing the full circle "ducky-ness" of the dish.

Finishing each element properly and in balance makes this bowl as delicious a tribute that we can create to the effort and love Erin and her family put into raising us these beautiful pastured animals.

INGREDIENTS

FOR THE DUCK

1 whole McIntosh Farms Muscovy duck, on the bone

FOR THE MERCER DUCK CURE

500 g (18 oz)	kosher salt
500 g (18 oz)	brown sugar
20 g (1 oz)	kimchi chili powder
10 g (0.5 oz)	five-spice powder
5 g (0.2 oz)	garlic powder

FOR THE CONFIT DUCK LEG

2	cured duck legs (see Mercer Duck Cure below)
2-4 L (about 8-16 cup)	rendered duck fat (can be reused many times to confit duck or other meats)
1	whole clove of garlic
2	bay leaves
5	sprigs of thyme

FOR THE VEGETABLES

1/2 lb (227 g)	heirloom carrots
1/2 lb (227 g)	Japanese eggplant
1/2 lb (227 g)	celery root
1/2 lb (227 g)	green zucchini
1 lb (455 g)	white onion

METHOD

THE DUCK

Yields 4 portions

Remove the legs from the duck and set aside. Remove the spine from the duck below the wings leaving the two breasts and wings together in one piece on the breast bone creating a "crown."

MERCER DUCK CURE

Yields 1 kg

Combine the cure ingredients thoroughly in a mixing bowl, then sprinkle on the duck pieces. (The cure can also be used on pork or chicken.) Rub the cure vigorously into both the legs and crowns of the duck and then let them sit uncovered over night on a rack in the refrigerator. The cure is the first step in building flavour, as well as the caramelization of the skin into the finished product. It is important to leave the crowns uncovered in the refrigerator so that the skin can dry out. While the duck cures make the sauces.

THE SAUCES

The sauce used to finish this bowl is a combination of two base sauces used in many dishes on the Mercer menu. If you don't want to make the sauces, use barbecue sauce of your choice and a seasoned soy sauce like ponzu. I recommend using the two sauce recipes below both to capture the authentic Mercer version of the dish as well as to have some great sauces in your pantry that you can use anytime you like.

THE CONFIT DUCK LEG

Yields 4 portions

Preheat oven to 325F (163C).

After curing overnight, rinse any remaining cure off of the legs and pat dry. Warm up enough duck fat to cover the legs in a deep, oven-proof vessel until it is melted. Place the duck legs, garlic, bay leaves and thyme into the vessel and place on the centre rack of the oven. After about 30 minutes the fat should be heated to a "lazy simmer" with just a few bubbles popping up every couple of seconds. Adjust the temperature of the oven to maintain this level of cooking (boiling the duck legs in the fat will result in tough meat). After 1-1/2 hours, test the duck leg for tenderness with a skewer: it should pierce the leg very easily and not feel any "grip" from the meat. Continue cooking gently until this degree of tenderness is reached. Remove the duck

legs from the fat when very tender and set aside to cool. Strain and keep the duck fat for future use. When cooled to handling temperature, separate the meat of the duck legs from the skin, bone and sinew. The meat will be in small chunks but try not to shred it too finely as it will disappear in the finished bowl. Reserve the confit duck leg meat in the fridge until ready to finish the bowl.

THE BREAST

Yields 4 portions

Preheat oven to 450F (230C).

Brush the remaining cure off of the duck crown. Remove as much as possible while resisting the urge to rinse the duck because keeping the skin dry is very important to the final colour. Place the duck crown in the oven for 15 minutes (the goal is to start browning the duck without cooking it too far). Drop the oven temp to 300F (150C) after the 15 minutes. Using a probe thermometer, take the temperature of the duck breast in the centre of the thickest part. When it has reached 100F (38C) internal temperature, remove it from the oven. The crown will still be very raw but the skin should have begun to caramelize. Cool the crown completely in the fridge. When cool remove the two breasts from the crown by carefully slicing either side of the keel bone at the centre of the crown, straight down to the breast plate. With your free hand, gently peel the duck breast away from the keel bone, breast plate and rib cage as you use a sharp boning knife to release the meat. It is important to keep the blade of the knife directed at the bone and make smooth cuts as you release the breast to get maximum yield. As you reach the wing of the crown and the breast muscle is detached, you can cut through the skin on the lower side of the breast to free it completely from the crown. Repeat for the opposite breast. Return the breasts to the refrigerator and use the leftover bones and wings to make a delicious stock for another recipe of your choice.

Prepare a "hot smoker" by placing a vessel deep and wide enough to fit a wire rack and the duck breasts on the stove with a few hickory or apple wood chips on the bottom of the pan. Place a wire rack over the chips, ideally 2-inches (5 cm) or more from the base of the vessel. Place the chilled duck breast on the rack, cover the vessel with a snug lid and then turn the burner onto medium heat. After 1 to 2 minutes the chips will begin to smoulder filling the vessel with smoke. Turn the burner down to low so that the chips do not ignite. Keep the duck in the vessel with the smoke for 6 to 8 minutes to give them a light smokey flavour. Remove the breasts and return them to the fridge (they should still be very raw).

Carefully dispose of the smouldering chips by soaking them in water. They are a fire hazard if thrown directly into a garbage can after use. The breasts are now ready to be finished during the final assembly of the bowl.

THE VEGETABLES
Yields 4 portions

This blend of vegetables was chosen for the dish because they lend lots of varied colours, flavours and textures when stir-fried. The carrots, onions and celery root are also items that we can buy from local produce suppliers' cellars during Stratford's long winters. This helps keep vegetable farming a profitable venture for more months of the year.

Using a mandolin or sharp chef's knife, julienne all the vegetables into 2 to 4-inch (6 to 10 cm) lengths. Mix them in a large bowl and set aside until ready to finish the dish.

TO FINISH THE DISH
Yields 4 portions

Gather all elements

  The duck breasts

  Canola oil for stir-frying

  The vegetables

  Kosher salt

  The shredded confit duck leg

  Sesame oil

  Mercer Soy BBQ sauce

  Mercer Chilli Soy sauce

  4 McIntosh farm duck eggs

  4 portions hot cooked white rice
  (at Mercer we use a medium grain
  sushi rice)

  Thinly sliced green onion (slice on
  a bias for maximum length)

  Cilantro (washed and picked into
  small sprigs)

  Black sesame seeds

Pre-heat the broiler to high.

Place the duck breasts on an oven-safe tray under the broiler skin side up. The skin will begin to sizzle and brown. The goal is a crisp golden brown finish, not burnt. The flesh of the duck breast will begin to first heat up and then cook. The goal is to have the meat reach medium rare 135F (57C) at the same moment the skin is crisp and golden brown. Control this process by moving the breast closer or further from the broiler or flipping the breast flesh side up as needed.

Meanwhile, on the stove heat a wok or large skillet over high heat. Add 2 to 3 tablespoons of canola oil. Add the vegetables and season with kosher salt. Toss the vegetables in the pan until they begin to soften. Add the confit duck leg meat and toss the pan contents continuously. Add 2 tablespoons sesame oil (the flavour is key to the dish) and toss. Add 150 to 200 ml (about 2/3 cup) of Mercer Soy BBQ Sauce and 150 to 200 ml (about 2/3 cup) of Mercer Chili Soy Sauce. Toss until the sauces and oil combine to coat the vegetables and confit duck. Keep warm over low heat. Add small amounts of water or BBQ sauce as necessary to adjust the texture of the mixture.

Remove the cooked duck breast from the oven and rest for 3 to 5 minutes. In a non-stick skillet heat 4 tablespoons of canola oil over medium-high heat. Crack the duck eggs into the skillet and cook until the bottoms are well set. Place the skillet under the broiler to cook the top surface of the egg white while leaving the yolk runny.

To finish the dish, build a base in four rice bowls with hot rice. Divide the vegetable, sauce and confit mixture between the four bowls. The bowl should be saucy but not soupy. Place the duck breasts horizontally on a cutting board, skin side down (it is easier to slice this way). Slice vertically across both breasts from one end to the other in slices about 1/2-inch (1 cm) thick (a breast will usually yield between 10 and 12 slices). Divide the breast between the four bowls, skin side up, arranging them attractively on one side of the bowl on top of the rice and vegetable mixture. On the other side of the bowl, place a cooked duck egg sunny side up.

Garnish each bowl with a generous amount of sliced green onion and cilantro. Sprinkle a pinch of black sesame seeds over the finished dish.

Enjoy! At Mercer we have a very hardworking team of dedicated people executing this dish together seven days a week. If you made it this far in the recipe by yourself, you have more than earned your feast as well as paid respect to McIntosh Farms "lovingly raised" ducks.

MERCER SOY BBQ SAUCE

Yield 2L

INGREDIENTS

265 g (9 oz)	mirin (sweet Japanese cooking wine)
315 g (11 oz)	tamari (gluten free soy sauce)
640 g (23 oz)	tomato ketchup
265 g (9 oz)	unseasoned rice wine vinegar
35 g (1 oz)	kosher salt
35 g (1 oz)	dry mustard powder
35 g (1 oz)	chili powder
35 g (1 oz)	smoked paprika
435 g (15 oz)	brown sugar
120 g (4 oz)	lemon juice

METHOD

Combine all ingredients (except the brown sugar and lemon juice) in a large saucepan. Make sure to whisk vigorously to avoid the dried spices lumping up. Bring to a simmer, over medium-high heat. Reduce heat to medium-low and allow to simmer for 1 to 2 hours (until the volume has reduced to a thicker sauce texture). Add the brown sugar and whisk until dissolved. Simmer for a further 30 minutes stirring frequently to prevent burning. Remove from the heat, add the lemon juice and mix well to combine. Store Mercer Soy BBQ Sauce in the refrigerator.

MERCER CHILI SOY SAUCE

Yield 1.5L

INGREDIENTS

600ml	tamari
300ml (1-1/3 cup)	water
150ml (2/3 cup)	mirin
150ml (2/3 cup)	unseasoned rice wine vinegar
1/4 cup	brown sugar
1 Tbsp	Piri Piri hot sauce (replace with Franks if you can't find Piri Piri)
15 g (0.5 oz)	cornstarch
15 g (0.5 oz)	water

METHOD

Combine all ingredients (except for the cornstarch and water) in a medium saucepan and bring to a simmer, over medium heat, for 20 minutes, whisking frequently. In a small mixing bowl, whisk together the cornstarch and water to form a slurry and add it the simmered sauce. Whisk vigorously to combine, then allow the mixture to come back to a boil. The sauce should thicken as it boils. Remove from the heat, cool and store in the refrigerator.

THE RED RABBIT

Sean Collins

Two years of architecture engineering at Conestoga College after high school didn't quite capture Sean Collins's interest, but the design of cooking did: there's a technical discipline in both fields he finds satisfying. "Design appeals to me. It's something I'm very aware of and try to get better at." That attention to detail and precision could partly explain why he enrolled in the Chefs School in 2005 and why he has remained focussed on farm-to-table now. There is, of course, a culinary precedent for the direct line drawn from the aesthetics of architecture to those of fresh and local farm-to-table through Jeremiah Tower and Chez Panisse. "It's designing something that looks nice without it looking like you tried to make it look nice," says Collins of his cooking at The Red Rabbit. The four-year-old restaurant captures a simple aesthetic, with a casual setting, some bar seating, craft beer, and food that he describes as rustic Canadian. "It's straightforward. We want to comfort people visually and with taste."

Being involved with the school and like-minded people when he arrived in Stratford allowed him to explore possibilities. "We started paying attention to what restaurants were doing elsewhere. You have to start pushing the envelope if you want to get noticed. I think the school was hugely influential in that." He also recognizes that farm-to-table is dictated by basic economics – the laws of supply and demand. "I have relationships with several local farmers, but I can't use all of them all year round because we can only sell so many plates of food in a week. We switch from season to season, and it's important to keep a dialogue going with them even when you're not getting products from them." He might use four or five pork producers, each delivering a different product. It gives the kitchen the opportunity to learn by going to the farm and seeing first hand. "Do they love what they're doing? For me, that's the first step. Farmers and producers putting love into their products are going to be creating something delicious."

In fact, diversity is part of design: the heterogeneity of farm-to-table encourages culinary exploration and creativity; it demands flexibility. Perhaps, because of the nature of the tomatoes or the fat in the pork, the dish you were going to do has to change and you have to adjust quickly to something different. "You have to be ready to roll with it," Collins says. "You set those expectations when you open a restaurant," but adds that another challenge with farm-to-table is cost. "We're producing goods of the quality we love and enjoy and that may not be aligned with people's perception of what they should be paying at a restaurant or a market. But the more restaurants doing it, the easier it gets," he says of the burgeoning farm-to-table dynamic in the county. "You have to attract a wide scope of customers, but I'd love to see more shops opening that are doing one or two things really well."

CHURCH HILL FARM

Max Lass

The lower portion of the farmhouse screen door is scrolled with "CHF"; the upper offers a tight, spyglass view through the first floor to the rolling acres of the 1850s Church Hill Farm that lie beyond. Inside the large open kitchen, the view is sweeping: barns, farm equipment, bush, and woodlot, some ducks and a few dozen sheep wending their ovine, ruminant way through the grass. Max Lass turns from the stove and gazes out the window. He's cooking burgers made with vache Canadienne beef, a unique French-Canadian breed with which he's currently experimenting. The heat under control, the pops and sizzles in the frying pan are calm as the fat renders. Lass is calm too, though he's been without sleep lately, he says. "The dogs help keep the coyotes away, but the barking also keeps us awake at night."

Lambing at three a.m. tends to ruin your sleep too. After 15 years at Church Hill, and after a previous life as a dairy farmer – where, he says, "there's only one thing to do all year" – he's enjoyed the variety, the problem solving, of the animals and this business. But he's also contemplating a succession plan for his kids – just not the meat business; that's his pride, nurtured nicely in Perth County and Waterloo Region. "The business grew one restaurant at a time, starting with The Prune and Bryan Steele. He had such a great reputation that he'd just phone a chef and say you should try this Church Hill meat. It went from there," Lass says. Steele, a chef school instructor, is part of the farm-to-table milieu that Lass says is pivotal to the local food scene. "They train chefs to understand what farmers are doing. Here, we give the animals a natural approach to life. We don't agree with feedlot production or raising chickens or ducks in a per-square-foot environment. Pork isn't just pork," he says emphatically. "Pigs are forest creatures. They need to be outside eating roughage, vegetables, roots, and tubers."

That approach has defined Church Hill Farm within the farm-to-table landscape, where there is a table-to-farm element too: vegetable trimmings from restaurants and brewers' mash from craft beer producers travel back to the farm as a source of food for Lass's animals. "We get restaurant scraps and trimmings," he says. "They keep it in the refrigerator, and I pick it up three times a week." It's a closed loop of producer and chef: the farmhouse kitchen plays a role when Lass cooks for the chefs who have cooked for him. "We reciprocate. They come here, and we cook them a nice meal and hang out for an afternoon. We have lots to talk about when it comes to food." Between bites of burger and sips of local English pale ale, Lass reflects, perhaps about his kids. He's not wistful talking about the past – or about the future – but he is candid. "This isn't growing fast," he says of the farm-to-table movement. "I look at Europe and how consumers buy fresh every day and appreciate good food – and will pay for it. Maybe someday that will happen here to a greater degree."

CHARCOAL-GRILLED CHURCH HILL FARM LAMB WITH HERBS AND FREEKEH

INGREDIENTS

1	fresh boneless free-range lamb leg, butterflied
1/4 cup	pepper, fresh ground
1/4 cup	cumin, toasted and ground
3 Tbsp	butter
6 oz (170g)	pancetta or cured pork, small dice
1	large onion, minced
8	cloves fresh garlic, minced
	Freekeh* (or farro), cooked like pasta in boiling salted water until tender, cooled
	kosher salt
1	lemon (for juice and zest)
2	eggs
1/2 cup	panko bread crumbs
1/2 cup	chopped fresh herbs (use whatever herbs you like!)
	olive oil to rub meat

TO FINISH THE DISH

Sugar snap peas	Mustard
Butter	Feta, crumbled

(*freekeh is harvested grains from green durum wheat that is roasted and dried to create its unique smoky flavour.)

EQUIPMENT NEEDED

Charcoal grill, fire pit, or propane barbecue
Good quality charcoal
Butcher twine
Probe thermometer

METHOD

The night before prepare the lamb: spread lamb out on a cutting board or sheet pan and season generously with pepper and cumin on all sides. Return the seasoned lamb to the fridge and let it sit for 2-12 hours (roll it up to save space).

To make the stuffing, add the butter to a large skillet and cook over medium heat until just bubbling. Add the pancetta and cook until lightly crisp. Add the onion and garlic and cook until translucent. Add the cooked freekeh, salt and pepper and lemon. Remove from the heat and let cool slightly. Stir in the eggs, panko and fresh herbs and taste to adjust seasoning as needed. Refrigerate overnight.

The next day, light the charcoal and let it burn until it has created a nice bed of coals in a charcoal barbecue or fire-pit with a rack. Have a second pile of burning charcoal ready to replenish the fire, if needed. If using propane, preheat the grill to medium heat. In the meantime, finish the lamb. Remove meat and stuffing from the fridge and spread the lamb onto a metal tray or in a roasting pan. Season generously with salt. Spoon the stuffing in a row slightly off the centre of the meat to form a cylinder, almost from end to end. Roll the meat over and shape it into a cylinder with the seam on the bottom. Tie the cylinder tightly with 4 or 5 pieces of butcher twine, tucking any stuffing back into the cylinder. Season the outside of the meat with salt, rub lightly with olive oil and set aside.

When your grill is hot enough that you can't hold your hand over for 5 seconds, carefully place lamb roast on the grill. Grill on all sides until golden brown and slightly charred (about 2-4 minutes per side). With a probe thermometer, check internal temperature every 10-15 minutes. Roast until the thermometer reaches 135-145F (57-63C). If internal temperature is not reached and the surface of the meat is getting too dark, simply push coals to one side and continue cooking over indirect heat until finished. If using a propane barbecue, turn burners off on one side and move lamb to that side and close the lid. Remove the roast to a platter, cover with foil and let it rest for 15 to 30 minutes (or longer). Remove the string and carve the lamb with your sharpest knife. Serve with fresh sugar snap peas sautéed in butter, your favourite mustard and crumbled local feta.

THE COMMON

Tim Otsuki

As 2017 was winding down to a close, Tim Otsuki opened a 40-seat restaurant in Stratford called The Common. It was an answer to a simple question he had been thinking about: do I live to work, or work to live? In a previous life, the Stratford-born Otsuki had spent time in mechanical engineering – and at a job that prompted him to ask the question in the first place. "After a couple of years, I realized it wasn't for me, so I re-evaluated. I had a philosophy that I would work so I could have the lifestyle I wanted, but I was working and not enjoying myself. Now I spend time doing something that I really like doing," he says. Restaurants had been part of his youth, and he'd had part-time jobs washing dishes and busing tables, he says. "Later, I had a friend who had a restaurant in Toronto. My first shift there I was hooked and have never looked back." He returned to Stratford a year later and enrolled in the school, graduating in 2002. That ending was also a starting point for an enlightening decade of travel and work abroad. "Every culture has its comfort food, I've found. In Hong Kong, the kitchen I worked in called it second dinner, and they'd take me out for the food they wanted to eat after service." Such experiences make The Common "pretty eclectic," Otsuki says. "There are dishes from quite a few different places." He pauses, then adds that the school helped his vision with a foundation in French and Italian cookery as well as in the foods of other nations. "If I recall, at that time Baxter was really into Moroccan cooking so that training is what I've built on in my career."

Like his restaurant's menu, Otsuki describes the Stratford restaurant scene as evolving. "It's driven by customers. Where it used to be fine dining, it's moved to more casual. The world is smaller and people know more about foods from different countries. As a kid, I remember my mother travelling to Toronto to get Japanese produce because you couldn't get it here. Today you can." At any time, Otsuki might have ingredients, both conventional and unique, from Loco Fields, Soiled Reputation, and Churchill Farm on the menu. "Max once came to me with this huge pork loin from a Mangalitsa pig he had slaughtered," he says. "You have to use local, fresh ingredients because they're just better." With ingredients and experiences aligned, Otsuki states that foods produced on the same latitude go well together. "I try to be true to place of origin, but my experience tells me otherwise. I'll mix a conch recipe from the Caribbean with a southeast Asian sauce, and it's fantastic." So while he's clearly enjoying what he's doing, he says there's still a lot of food to explore. "I said the world is small, but there's so much of it I haven't seen. You'd have to live a thousand years to learn all there is to learn about cooking."

TEA LEAVES

Karen Hartwick

For most of its time as an after-dinner beverage in restaurants, a cup of tea has been an anticlimax, according to tea expert Karen Hartwick. "There's this amazing dining experience with fantastic local foods, a wide range of cooking techniques from around the world, and extensive wine and scotch lists. And then they offer you a tea bag. There's a disconnect there," asserts Hartwick. Tea, however, is a growing component of food service, and Hartwick's role has been to educate. After a time in western Canada in the fashion industry, the London, Ontario-born Hartwick moved to Stratford with camellia sinensis on her mind. "The tea bug had hit me." She trained at the Specialty Tea Institute in New York City – which made her Canada's first tea sommelier – and opened Tea Leaves Tasting Bar in an 1880s Victorian manor on Erie Street. "It has Zen and a calm energy," Hartwick says, which is what you'd expect of a tea shop. She's travelled the tea-producing regions of the world and has shared her knowledge with Stratford Chefs School students for nearly a decade. "They start to realize the exotic nature of tea and the possible flavours." Early on, Hartwick also provided tea for Rundles restaurant, an opportunity that started her wholesale business so that now many Stratford restaurants serve her teas, making it a city that has embraced tea culture. "I love the fact that you can come to Stratford and try different styles of food at different restaurants and now tea is a part of that experience."

Like wine, tea can be tailored to a restaurant's menu. "We look at what style of tea fits the business," Hartwick says, "and match it with the food. We provide familiar choices but also introduce customers to something unique when it comes to tea." In keeping with the collaborative nature of the local food and beverage industry, Hartwick trains restaurant staff in tasting and serving tea, and introduces them to the untapped potential of tea as a cooking ingredient. "It's still a baby in North America," she says. "In tea-producing countries, they use the green leaf right off the plant in their cooking, but you can't do that here because of limited access to the raw leaf." She cites Ryan O'Donnell of Mercer Kitchen as a chef who has used tea inventively in a collaborative dinner. "Every course was cooked with tea, and it was amazing," she says, pointing out tea's versatility from smokey lapsang or toasted Japanese teas that have roasted rice in them to teas that work in sweet and savoury desserts. We think of collaboration between farmers and chefs, but select ingredients like tea, though they are not local, play a role, too: it's the school that is the tie that binds. "It instills passion and work ethic in students," according to Hartwick. "The skills they learn come into play here but they also head off to other communities. Maybe they'll end up opening their own restaurant, maybe not. But the school is key to these young chefs starting off."

SALMON WITH MISO, GINGER, AND LIQUORICE GLAZE

MAKES 4 SERVINGS OF SALMON

This recipe is a variation on one of my mother's recipes. I have used Ginger Liquorice tea from Tea Leaves as an element of the salmon glaze, but one could also use Tea Leaves matcha for a variation on flavour.

INGREDIENTS

1/4 cup	blonde miso paste
1 Tbsp	mirin
3 Tbsp	sugar
1 Tbsp	sake
1 Tbsp	shoyu
1/2 tsp	sesame oil
2 Tbsp	Tea Leaves Ginger Liquorice tea, brewed strongly
4	salmon fillet pieces (about 4 ounces (113 g) each)
	vegetable oil, as required
1 tsp	white sesame seeds
1	green onion, thinly sliced

METHOD

Preheat oven to 450F (232C).

In a small mixing bowl combine miso, mirin, sugar, sake, shoyu, sesame oil, ginger liquorice tea and stir until sugar dissolves. Reserve.

Bake salmon in a heavy skillet, drizzled with a little vegetable oil, until it turns a light pink in colour (about 5 minutes).

Remove salmon from oven, cover salmon pieces with reserved miso glaze, sprinkle with sesame seeds, green onions, and continue to cook until glaze caramelizes (about 2 to 3 more minutes).

TO FINISH THE DISH

Serve salmon as desired. We like it with ginger rice pilaf and vegetables tossed in teriyaki sauce.

KEYSTONE ALLEY

Tina Logassi

Brantford born and Barrie raised, Tina Logassi got an early start cooking, even if it swerved into the automotive sector for a time. "I was in the kitchen baking when I was three and got my first pasta roller when I was 13," Logassi says. "But I pursued math and sciences in high school like they tell you to and worked in automotive engineering for eight years." The crash of 2008 – what she calls a "blessing" – sent her down another avenue when car manufacturing went into a tailspin. "It was a chance to switch careers, and I enrolled at Stratford." She worked at Pazzo after graduating and was part of the team that opened Mercer Hall, before working as a sous chef on an exclusive private yacht cooking for organizations like National Geographic and Scripps Institution of Oceanography. She's been chef at Keystone Alley since 2016.

Acknowledging those who say formal training for chefs is unnecessary, she maintains that education gives young cooks fundamental skills and basic knowledge – and a lot more. "It gives history, context. I think people need to know who Paul Bocuse was and what he contributed. We need to think about where a dish came from and what and how we're cooking today. That's extremely important, as is the science of cooking and why this works and why this doesn't." As for students working faster, more efficiently and precisely, she says that's the role of the kitchen. "It's hours of practice and work."

Logassi says Stratford is a blend of blue collar and agriculture with an evolving restaurant culture. "It's exciting that a town this size has so many restaurants, and many of us really try to support local, but that's not the case everywhere." At the same time she says she works with producers and growers such as McIntosh Farm, A Still, Small Farm, Monforte, and Perth Pork Products, she adds a caveat: "It's tricky dealing with 12 different people, and it might be that one week you're short of produce. It's more work from the chef's perspective to make it happen, but it's worth it." To add their own hyper-local element, Keystone grows tomatoes, radishes, and micro greens, and even brews its own beer on-site. And while Logassi believes local can be cheaper and her chef school training says it's key to "work from scratch," she's realistic about the demands of time and money. "I'm at a point where we're needing to spend less time breaking down products, so I'm working with Fred [de Martines of Perth Pork Products] to get loins that don't need someone to deal with them in terms of butchery." They were once breaking down 60 chickens from McIntosh Farm in a week and ran wing specials because they didn't know what to do with them. The process was too much work, so she arranged with Erin McIntosh to buy just chicken breasts. "That saved a lot of labour," Logassi says. "And producers willing to be flexible will get further faster too."

A STILL, SMALL FARM

Andrew Courtney

His land provides him an income, but it's also something he studies constantly: after a decade of farming, Andrew Courtney wants to know more. "It's all about the soil," he says. "It's an entire world, and I want to learn more." The owner of A Still, Small Farm – the name playing on permanence and the quiet, tranquil nature of the farm – Courtney works about two acres of Perth County's light clay soil growing what he calls "salad crops." He sells salad subscriptions that include greens, cucumbers, tomatoes, and peppers to residents in Stratford and the surrounding area, but he works with food operations too. His strategy is to keep the acreage tight: the low tillage approach, few farm hands, and low overhead is a farming model Courtney says is gaining in popularity; it's suited him well. "If you have a good relationship with your landlord, which I do, and they believe in what you're doing, there is security." In fact, though it's counter-intuitive, he's given himself the target of meeting his financial goals on less land. "In three years, I'd like to use a third of this land and just get better and better with what I'm growing." While honing skills and knowledge, growing a customer base, and seeking efficiencies are the nuts and bolts of any business, Courtney is also motivated by the intrinsic value of his craft. "Farming is something I believe in. For most of human history, we've been in the field, so it's nothing new. It's humbling to work in the dirt and at the end of the day you know you're doing something that people need. So that's good."

The salad subscription – his goal is 250 members – starts in mid-June and runs until November, and he says it's a unique venture. "I don't know of many others. The commitment to the subscription is necessary, but it's also nice if you are interested in what's going on at the farm." At the same time, he sells produce to Keystone Alley, The Pulp, and AO Pasta, which requires a different approach than selling subscriptions. "The home cook cares less about leaf size," he says. He then points to kale that could be destined for Keystone Alley – "last year they made kale chips," he notes – explaining that the rows of plants are covered during vulnerable times in their growth. "Pests like eating something that isn't healthy. And sow thistle is another problem that I need to learn more about. It spreads under the ground, and it's scary." Courtney grows crops that don't need a lot of weeding, another trial and error process he's learned on the job. "The healthier the soil, the less pressure from pests. It's all about balance and feeding the particular crop what it needs." He pauses for a moment before he adds that his contribution helps make Stratford unique when it comes to food. "It's a place where a lot of people come for special occasions, but I want to focus on people's kitchen tables at home. I want this to be fresh and affordable."

RED KALE AND BRUSSELS SPROUTS SALAD

INGREDIENTS

FOR THE SALAD

3 parts kale, chopped (a 1/4-inch (0.6 cm) width chop improves texture of the kale)

1 part Brussels sprouts, thinly sliced

1 part red cabbage, thinly sliced

FOR THE LEMON-POPPY SEED DRESSING

6 Tbsp	freshly squeezed lemon juice
1/2 tsp	onion powder
1 tsp	dijon mustard
1/2 tsp	salt
4 1/2 Tbsp	sugar
1/2 cup (125 ml)	canola oil (or any neutral-flavoured oil)
1 Tbsp	poppy seeds

FOR THE CANDIED SUNFLOWER SEEDS

2 Tbsp	maple syrup
2 Tbsp	corn syrup
2 Tbsp	sugar
1/4 tsp	salt
1 cup	sunflower seeds

TO FINISH THE DISH

Feta cheese, crumbled

Dried cranberries (you can substitute dried apricots, cherries, etc.)

METHOD

LEMON-POPPY SEED DRESSING

Combine the lemon juice, onion powder, mustard, salt, and sugar in a large mixing bowl and whisk together well. Slowly pour in the oil and incorporate. Stir in the poppy seeds.

Recipe notes: Dressing will keep a week in the fridge. For the Brussels sprouts and cabbage, you can finely chop by hand or use a thin slicing attachment on a food processor. The salad mix can be made ahead of time. Keep it in a sealed container in the fridge for up to a week.

CANDIED SUNFLOWER SEEDS

Preheat oven to 375F (190C). Combine syrups, sugar, and salt together in bowl. Add sunflower seeds and stir together thoroughly. Spread the mixture thinly on a parchment-lined baking sheet. Bake for 4 to 8 minutes. Depending on your oven, it could take longer. You will see the seeds bubbling rapidly, but when the bubbling slows, they are done. The process can happen quickly, so watch carefully to avoid burning them. Allow the seeds to cool on the baking sheet. The coating should be crisp when cooled. If not, return them to the oven and continue cooking a couple of minutes more.

Recipe notes: The seeds will keep a couple of weeks in a sealed container on the counter. Try substituting pumpkin seeds, walnuts, pecans, or a mixture.

SALAD

To a good-sized salad bowl, add the salad mix and pour in some lemon-poppyseed dressing. The kale can hold up to it, so you can be generous in applying the dressing. Add the candied sunflower seeds, feta cheese and dried cranberries. If you buy the feta that comes in brine, it's delicious if you spoon a bit of the salty brine into the salad as well.

PIZZA BISTRO | WELLINGTON STREET INN

Tom Giannakopoulos

After his first year at the Stratford Chefs School, Tom Giannakopoulos said, "I now know what I don't know." The 22-year-old graduate has cooking experience gained through his family's restaurants in Stratford, the city in which he grew up. "From the time I was 13 years old, I've been working in restaurants," Giannakopoulos says, adding that attending the school was a natural progression from what he'd already been doing. What might be called serial entrepreneurs in the food and hospitality industry, his family's current business is Pizza Bistro, along with its four boutique suites, and has been operating for five years. It's small business in the truest sense of the phrase. "It's my father and I," Giannakopoulos says. "We work as a two-man team in the kitchen. It's a pizzeria and a bistro where we do Greek-style cooking with some other Mediterranean influences. It's a niche we've tried to pick out for ourselves." Rather than stick strictly to only traditional recipes, Giannakopoulos says they're influenced by flavours, too. "We don't call ourselves a traditional Greek restaurant, so that leaves us with lots of room for creative thinking to come up with any dish we want."

Giannakopoulos sees his time at the school as having provided him with key components for building his skills and understanding business. "The school teaches you how to be a restaurateur, from the theory classes to the cooking classes. You're being exposed to things you haven't seen before and classical techniques. It gave me a very good foundation." Another benefit he says he sees as part of his education is the connection between the chef-instructors and local food businesses that are part and parcel of the infrastructure that exists between the school and the city. "As a student, you build up relationships and meet so many other people, including the chefs-in-residence." Stratford as a dining culture he describes as similarly connected and dynamic, where a lot of chefs work with producers in and around the area. He himself is an example: he heads to the Sunday morning Slow Food Market on a regular basis. "Right now, we're getting beautiful cherry tomatoes, corn, and carrots, for instance. We also might get some pork. All the produce is grown very close by, and we get to see exactly what we're buying. There are alumni who work year-round and are very familiar with the area, and there's a rapport and relationships that are built around the products." Those connections and the quality they make their priority has encouraged people who love good food to visit the city and its restaurants, according to Giannakopoulos. He's motivated by that energy and his culinary training to apply it to the family business to help it grow. "I think we're doing something different in Stratford. You have to do something different here because there is such an abundance of restaurants and such good chefs that you need to be unique. I feel that we are and will continue moving in that direction."

THE BUTCHER AND THE BAKER

Rick Frank

According to Rick Frank, the difference between butchery and meat-cutting highlights what he sees as a weakness in our food system. "Butchery is slowly turning into a lost art, certainly in Ontario," Frank says. The Kitchener-born Frank owns and operates The Butcher and the Baker on Wellington Street in downtown Stratford, a specialty food shop that is at once a butcher, a baker (baking about 15 different breads on-site daily), a greengrocer, and more. As a butcher, Frank trained in the old-European style, having worked at Schneiders on Courtland Avenue in Kitchener, an enormous empty shell of a building being demolished so the land can be re-developed – a certain sign of a changing industry. "I learned from butchers trained in the traditional way, and they learned from the butchers before them," says Frank. During a recent late-summer trip to Switzerland for a family wedding, he found the ancient craft alive and well. Though he describes the devolution of the trade here as sad, he says he's not bitter – his store is quite busy, in fact – and neither is he being nostalgic. Rather, Frank simply says when it comes to butchery, we could do better. "When I came to Stratford, there were four butchers. I'm the last remaining. In Europe, it's still considered an important trade and requires years of training to become a master butcher." The store does its own butchery and makes a significant portion of what butchers have traditionally made: fresh sausage, terrines, and some cold cuts, among others. "We make what

the government allows us to make. Anything we buy is locally sourced."

Frank, who in the past instructed Chefs School students in aspects of butchery, has guided his business through several iterations in its time, and they've been at the current location for about a dozen years. But he says the decades have seen the butchery trade shrink and make it harder for similar businesses to survive. Regulations have tightened and inspection authorities have changed. "It makes it more difficult to make money when you can't make all the products yourself. We have the means, we're just not allowed." Admitting that he'd love to see traditional-style butchery "resurrected," he's moved on. "It's sad that it doesn't exist the way it used to," he says. "I'm not really sure how you address that – or if anyone really wants to. I can survive here because this is a wonderful town that supports local food businesses. That doesn't happen everywhere." The Butcher and the Baker has evolved and thrived, and Frank loves the city and the food culture of which he is a part. "The Stratford food scene is quite dynamic with an incredible variety of restaurants for such a small town, more in the core than even much larger cities like Kitchener," he says. Part of that vitality must be attributed to the city's cultural institutions, for which he's thankful. "That's what's beautiful about Stratford. I think the Festival and the Chefs School really play an important part."

SLOW BRAISED LAMB SHANKS IN A SPICED RED WINE BROTH

Makes about 15 servings

INGREDIENTS

LAMB SHANKS INGREDIENTS

15 lamb shanks, bone-in (we like the ones from The Butcher and the Baker)

Olive oil, as required

Salt and freshly ground black pepper, as required

4 Tbsp	dried oregano
4	onions, peeled and roughly chopped
20	whole garlic cloves, peeled
1 bunch	rosemary
1 bunch	thyme
4 Tbsp	ground cinnamon
3 Tbsp	ground cumin
2 Tbsp	ground clove
1 Tbsp	Spanish paprika
8	whole cardamom pods
5	whole star anise
3/4	bottle of red wine
6 cups (1-1/2 L)	canned tomato purée
4 cups (1 L)	water
2	cinnamon sticks
5	bay leaves

ORZO PILAF INGREDIENTS

2 packages of dried orzo pasta

Lamb braising liquid (from above)

Butter, cubed

Parmesan cheese

TO FINISH THE DISH

Seasonal vegetables of your choice (we like roasted root vegetables, green beans, and rapini)

Parsley, chopped

Parmesan cheese

METHOD

LAMB SHANKS METHOD

Preheat your oven to 500F (260C).

Place the lamb shanks into a baking dish large enough to hold them all in a single layer without crowding them. Drizzle some olive oil over the lamb shanks and season them generously with salt, pepper, and 2 Tbsp of the dried oregano. Roast lamb shanks until they are brown on all sides (about 40 minutes).

Meanwhile, heat a large saucepan over medium-high heat, add the onion, garlic, rosemary, and thyme. Season with salt, pepper, the remaining 2 tablespoons of dried oregano, reduce heat to medium and cook until the onions are translucent (about 10 to 15 minutes). Once they are translucent add the cinnamon, cumin, clove, paprika, cardamom, and star anise and continue to gently cook the onions with the spices, scraping the bottom of the saucepan with a wooden spoon, until the spices are toasted and very aromatic (about 3 to 5 minutes). Add the red wine to deglaze the saucepan while you continue to scrape the bottom with a wooden spoon to loosen anything that has caramelized. Add the tomato purée and season again with salt and pepper.

Reduce the oven temperature to 350F (180C).

Remove lamb shanks from the oven. Deglaze the baking dish with 2 cups (500 ml) of water and move the lamb shanks around with a wooden spoon to loosen them up a bit. Add the spiced red wine braising liquid so that the lamb shanks are fully submerged (top up with remaining 2 cups (500 ml) water if necessary), then add the cinnamon sticks and bay leaves.

Cover the baking dish with aluminum foil and braise in the oven until the lamb shanks are very tender (at least 3 hours). Once the lamb is tender, carefully remove the lamb shanks from the baking dish and strain the braising liquid into a clean saucepan.

ORZO PILAF METHOD

In large saucepan of salted water cook the orzo pasta until it is al dente, strain and reserve.

In a second saucepan, combine cooked orzo with enough of the lamb shank braising liquid to moisten it and bring to a simmer over medium heat. Once the orzo comes to a simmer add butter and Parmesan to adjust consistency and taste to you liking. Season with salt and pepper and keep warm.

TO FINISH THE DISH

To reheat the lamb shanks, place them in the baking dish with some braising liquid and warm them in the oven. Spoon the Orzo Pilaf into the centre of your serving plates and place a lamb shank on top. Garnish with seasonal vegetables, freshly chopped parsley, and Parmesan cheese.

PAZZO PIZZERIA AND TAVERNA

Yva Santini

Yva Santini, a St. Marys, Ontario, native, started working in professional kitchens as a young teenager. Today, she's been cooking at Pazzo for 12 years, the last eight of which she has been chef. A 2009 graduate of the Stratford Chefs School, Santini says she knew after a couple of years that post-secondary study wasn't for her, at least in its traditional and static academic format. "I spent a couple of years at the University of Toronto as an undergraduate and realized that I wanted a career that was more hands-on." There was something attractive about what she calls the kinesthetics and physicality of cooking, but there was something more, she says. "I also wanted something creative." Cooking appeared to be the right path, especially since she'd gotten a strong foundation working several seasons with chef and Stratford Chefs School instructor Bryan Steele at The Prune. It gave her a lot of insight into the Chefs School. "It seemed like a natural choice, and I like living in Stratford. I think it's a vibrant community." Her restaurant experience as a member of that community has in fact shaped her understanding of the nature of the food landscape around her. "The general public has become more aware of what they want to eat and know more about where their food comes from," she says. "When I started, that was a niche market, but now it's exploded. It's something that is transparent and more common and has raised the bar for restaurants to fulfill the needs of that market."

She says the result has been more restaurants sourcing local and taking more care in choosing ingredients. The unique aspect of Stratford as a dining city and of Perth County as a home to local farms and producers, to Santini's thinking, is one of geography. "A lot of cities, including big cities like Toronto, feature local products, but producers are hours away. Our farms are very close to us. The products and the terroir here are superior and exceptional, and they're nearby."

Both current students and graduates are part of Pazzo's kitchen as they work with that terroir. The Chefs School, according to Santini, teaches the foundations and techniques that are essential to building a strong dining and restaurant scene, but it's not always the product – a graduate – that is the end result of the two years of hard work and study; there are intangibles in the process from which students benefit. "I gained the confidence that I can accomplish anything I set my mind to. The base set of skills I have allows me to approach something new no matter what it is. That confidence took years to develop, but I can meet any sort of issue in the restaurant." There's also the strong network of colleagues around her in the Stratford community. "The camaraderie among the chefs here is important, and there's healthy competition to continuously raise the bar for the whole community. That's been happening over the last ten years."

KAWTHOOLEI FARM ORGANICS

Pam Rogers

Each year, Pam Rogers has left her farm – Kawthoolei Farm Organics – during the long Stratford winters and headed for tropical climes. The 12,000-kilometer journey hasn't been to vacation but to work with the Karen people, refugees on the Thailand-Burma border. "I've been going there every year for five or six months at a time and have been doing that for 18 years. When I got the farm, I asked some of the Karen elders if I could use that name, which means 'land without evil.' There are quite a few people who have re-settled in Canada, and I wanted the farm to be open to them because my farm too is a land without evil," Rogers says. Near Cromarty, Ontario, the farm is home to 2,000 trees on 10 acres, of which she farms four and sells the produce at London's Covent Garden and at the Stratford Slow Food Market. "Otherwise," she says, "I sell to the chefs in Stratford. That's how I met Yva Santini at Pazzo." Kawthoolei produces a mix of vegetables, fruit, and herbs, both familiar and less so. "I grow about 50 different things," Rogers says with a laugh. Among her produce are Thai chili peppers, Dakota black popcorn, and organic strawberries, a difficult item to find, she says. Serving restaurants such as Pazzo, The Bruce, Bijou, and Red Rabbit among others, Rogers says her approach is unique too. "I don't have standing orders with chefs. I'm old-fashioned and when I have things I come around with them and let them know. If I have extra yellow beans, I'll take them around and ask if they want them. I like it that way. It's fun to go to the back door with the produce and say, 'Look what I've got.' I hope it lights up their imagination." The approach works: Kawthoolei has been in business for nine years, in good degree because Perth County chefs are focussed on local ingredients and look for unique products, according to Rogers. "I took some potatoes to The Bruce because they were looking for something specific that I grow. I try to find niches like that."

Stratford is special, she adds, because of the Chefs School and the creative environment around the theatre. "The chefs work within that culture, and they work together with each other and with farmers. We get to grow for some very skilled and talented people." For Rogers, that creativity – through farming – is healing, in light of her efforts on the Thai-Burma border. "There is so much trauma there and after working there so long I contain some of that. I find that being an organic farmer is grounding. It gives me a place to put all that sorrow, all that sadness, all that anger. Right into the ground. It's therapeutic and at the same time it carries on the creativity as a way to express myself."

[Note: In mid-September, Rogers represented Slow Food Perth County at Slow Food International Terre Madre Gusto in Turin, Italy. From there, she headed to the Thailand-Burma border.]

MELANZANE PARMIGIANA

This is a new addition to the Pazzo repertoire, and I have grown to be quite fond of it. It is the first vegetarian entrée that is not a pasta that I have put on a menu. Using Pam's organic produce exclusively to make this dish for this project was exciting and yielded a result most delicious! The San Marzano tomatoes and shallots from her farm made an outstandingly decadent tomato sauce. The texture of the eggplant was integral and the flavour was delicate. Something about it felt incredibly nourishing to eat. The four elements in this dish can all be prepared in advance. The tomato sauce, the basil pesto, and the la bomba are all sizeable enough recipes that you will have some leftover for your pantry to use as you please.

As a graduate of the Stratford Chefs School, I am always excited for the potential of working with new apprentices from the school. I tend toward promoting a kitchen environment that is particularly welcoming to first time cooks, and that also encourages an overall positive workspace for cooks of all skill levels. One of the many observations I have made in eight years working as a chef is that I can only achieve my goals if the kitchen works as a team. I have all of the apprentices and teammates that have worked with me in the past and currently to thank for shaping my culinary experience. So thank you, to all the teammates I have ever had and have now, I am very grateful!

INGREDIENTS

EGGPLANT

2	small Italian eggplants
	Diamond Crystal kosher salt
1/4 cup	all-purpose flour
2	eggs, beaten
1 cup	panko breadcrumbs
2 tsp	dried oregano
	Canola oil (for frying)

METHOD

EGGPLANT: 30 MINUTES

Peel and slice the eggplant into ½ inch (1.3 cm) rounds. Place the eggplant rounds in a large bowl and sprinkle with enough salt that you can see it sticking to each piece and not dissolving right away (about 2 to 4 tablespoons.) Toss the eggplant well in the salt and let sit for 20 minutes. After this time, you should observe a small pooling of water in your bowl. Rinse the eggplant in cold water thoroughly enough that when you squeeze the water out of the eggplant, it is salty enough to enjoy but not overly salty. If the water being squeezed out is too salty, keep rinsing. If the water is not salty at all, add more salt and let the eggplant sit again.

Once the eggplant is rinsed, set up the flour and the egg into two separate bowls, and the panko and oregano into a third. Dredge each piece of eggplant first in the flour, then the egg, then the panko mixture, ensuring the panko is being pushed in rather firmly to the eggplant. Set your eggplant aside until you are ready to fry and assemble the melanzane.

TOMATO SAUCE

1/2 cup	unsalted butter
4	medium sized shallots, diced
	salt and pepper and chili (optional) to taste
5 lbs	San Marzano tomatoes, cored and peeled
1/2 cup	canned whole tomato, hand crushed
1/4 cup	Parmigiano-Reggiano, shaved (for assembly)
3-5	thin slices of smoked mozzarella, or other melting cheese (for assembly)

BASIL PESTO

1/2 cup	mild tasting oil such as canola or grapeseed
1	small clove garlic
	salt and pepper to taste
1 cup	picked basil leaves, blanched, refreshed, and chopped
1/4 cup	Parmigiano-Reggiano, finely grated
	lemon juice to taste

MEAGHAN'S LA BOMBA

1/2	medium fennel bulb, chopped
1/2	small white onion, chopped
2	red bell pepper, seeded, chopped
1/4 cup	artichoke hearts, chopped
1/4 cup	green olives, pitted, chopped
1 cup	canola oil
1/2 cup	white wine vinegar
2 Tbsp	chilli flakes
	salt & pepper

TOMATO SAUCE: 1 HOUR 30 MINUTES; YIELD IS ROUGHLY 2 L

Choose a saucepan that will fit your ingredients into it, and begin by melting the butter. Add the diced shallots to the butter, season with salt and pepper, and cook until they are tender and sweet (about 8 to 10 minutes). Add the peeled and canned tomato and stir. Simmer this gently over low heat and stir with a wooden spoon frequently until the sauce reaches the desired consistency. Adjust the salt and pepper to your preference.

BASIL PESTO: 15 MINUTES

In a blender, add the oil, garlic, and some salt and pepper, and blend. Add the chopped basil and Parmigiano and blend ONLY until the basil becomes smooth and the colour a mostly homogeneous vibrant green colour with no specs. Taste the pesto and add salt, pepper, and lemon to your preference, and blend once more to incorporate your seasoning. Blending for too long may cause the pesto to heat and therefore discolour, so limit the duration of blending as much as possible.

MEAGHAN'S LA BOMBA

Place fennel, onion, red pepper, artichokes, olives, in a food processor. Pulse on and off for one minute, adding half the oil. Blitz for an additional 30 seconds, or until it is paste-like but still a little chunky. Remove and put into small saucepan. Add white wine vinegar, chilli flakes, remaining oil, and cook for 15 minutes on low heat. Season to taste.

ASSEMBLY: 15 MINUTES

Preset oven to 400F (200C)

In a high rimmed, heavy bottomed pot, add enough canola oil so that it is 2-inches (5 cm) deep and heat this gently to 375F (190C). Fry your eggplant rounds in this oil until they are a deep golden brown colour.

In an oven proof dish (sized for two portions) spoon in about one full cup of hot tomato sauce, and sprinkle the shaved Parmigiano on the sauce. Layer the fried eggplant on top of the sauce and distribute the la bomba and cheese however you desire. Bake until the cheese is melted. Garnish with basil pesto.

STRATFORD CHEFS SCHOOL TEAM MEMBERS, RECIPES & PERTH COUNTY PRODUCERS

INTRODUCTION

BY KIM COSGROVE

In 2013, when the Stratford Chefs School celebrated its 30th anniversary, we coined the phrase *"celebrating our past and anticipating our future"* in recognition not only of the major changes that were on the horizon for the school, but also to celebrate the vision, passion, creativity, and tenacity that were invested by its co-founders to be carried on by those who will manage the organization moving forward. It is this spirit that has sustained the Chefs School and inspired its alumni.

The following section profiles some of our alumni team members who work with the Chefs School during the professional program (which runs October through March). As with many alumni featured in this book, these individuals work at various restaurants throughout Stratford during the high tourist season (April through October).

A few of the profiles reflect members of our team that now work with us for the full year. These roles represent new programming initiatives and opportunities for the Chefs School as we enter into our 35th anniversary year.

Our new Open Kitchen programming offers recreational cooking classes, and culinary workshops, for the dedicated home cook. The loyally attended Springtime Weekend Cooking Class Retreats, once held at Rundles Restaurant, have moved into our facility and offer immersive, hands-on culinary experiences (from late March to early May). These experiences are a great way to meet new people, explore new cuisines, and have a lot of fun!

My deepest thanks go out to all members of the Stratford Chefs School community and especially to those who I have had the pleasure of working with over these past few years of intense transition which saw us build, and move into, a new year-round home after utilizing shared part-year facilities for more than 30 years.

ELI SILVERTHORNE

Stratford Chefs School & Open Kitchen

Eli Silverthorne works at the intersection of cookery and pedagogy. The London, Ontario, born Silverthorne has overseen the Stratford Chefs School "Open Kitchen" since December 2017, leading hands-on cooking classes for up to 14 home cooks and the food lover in general during the week at the school's 136 Ontario Street location. "Open Kitchen brings people in from the community, and they're surprised by how much they learn," says Silverthorne who has an undergraduate degree in History and Political Science at Western University. Yet, at the same time, he's surprised by how many Stratford residents are unfamiliar with the school; he sees that as an opportunity. "It's a way to be continuously involved with the community and opening up this space to them. It also allows us to create partnerships with other businesses and organizations."

The 2015 class valedictorian, Silverthorne has honed his communication skills in conjunction with his kitchen skills. "I saw that communication was essential, so I worked on those skills as an educational aide at Fanshawe College for about five years." He worked at The Prune during culinary school and after graduation and was on the team that helped Jonathan Gushue open The Berlin in Kitchener. Most recently, he has worked in the Mercer Hall kitchen in conjunction with the chef school. He says the school's impact is doubly important and help makes Stratford a culinary destination: "We graduate only a few people but they have significant influence," adding that the Open Kitchen can break down barriers elsewhere in the community. "People are pretty conservative in a lot of the things that they make and are apprehensive. We can demystify unfamiliar techniques and ingredients and show how flavourful celeriac or eggplant can be. And easy to prepare."

During the school term, Silverthorne teaches first-year practical cookery. "It pushes me. I know how to make risotto," he says, "but I'm always brushing up on things and being prepared for the unexpected question or understanding the science behind a technique, even if that question doesn't come up." He teaches to all his students that cooking is learning "project management" that utilizes all five senses. "It's a career that pushes you physically but also mentally. That's something that really drew me to it." When it comes to using local produce, he interprets that as meaning both using superior products and nurturing sustainability, especially when a farmer like Antony John visits restaurants to discuss tailoring what he grows for the kitchen's needs before it's even planted. "It's building a market rather than just hoping there will be one at the end and ensuring that producers have a viable income," says Silverthorne. "If they don't have revenue generated by local restaurants who care to showcase their product, we'll lose them. On an increasing basis, using local food is making more and more sense to more people. I hope it's not a trend but a lifestyle, even though we do live in a climate where a lot of the things we want to use can't be served year-round."

MOSS BERRY FARM

Ann Marie Moss

What started as her father's simple roadside fruit stand has grown into a robust business that spends six solid months making jam and chutney in their on-farm commercial kitchen in order to supply a year's worth of sales. Ann Marie Moss calls her father's farm, about 12 kilometers south of Stratford, her home farm and base of operations. "Back in the day, it was one of the first for pick-your-own strawberries, raspberries, gooseberries, and black currants," says Moss who runs the business with co-founder and co-owner husband Al Weber. Today, the company has been operating for two decades with the goal of producing old-time goodness. "We've been doing that for 20 years. We wanted to create a product that was as natural as possible and tastes like what your grandmother made," Moss says. "I think we've achieved that."

The food industry clearly made a mark on Moss. She studied hospitality at the University of Guelph and graduated from the Stratford Chefs School in 1992. "I always wanted to be a chef," she says. She apprenticed at Rundles and for a period taught the front-of-house service component at the school. As both a trained cook and a food manufacturer, she has a unique perspective on the history of Stratford's food. "The quality, variety, and diversity of what you can eat in a town of this size is on par with any place I've ever been to." She adds that at the local and national level, the school has provided the industry with chefs highly skilled in the basics of taste and cooking technique, along with the elements of entrepreneurship. "You can see that in the number of restaurants and food companies that have been opened by Stratford Chefs School grads," she says. In fact, she's the entrepreneurial proof: a couple of years ago, Moss Berry Farm began experimenting with the production of some new beverages. They concluded that what was old could be new again: they created a line of beverages – flavoured "tonics" – called switchels. If there is an irony in the choice of the switchel, a drink which traditionally combines a sweet component with ginger and vinegar, it is the fact that they drew the idea from its 18th century origins in order to attract a Millennial customer, says Moss. "Instead of coming up with more preserves, we wanted to appeal to a younger demographic. Someone suggested a ready-to-drink product, and we decided on switchels. We like old-time products that have a real history." Also called "haymakers' punch," the drink was designed for agricultural workers in the field, which nicely suits agrarian Perth County. "It was an original and natural energy drink," she says, and given the interest in food in the region – and the current kombucha craze – it supports her entrepreneurial claim for the school and the potential for the drink's reception. "There is a greater awareness of and appreciation for local products now than there was. I think the value that local producers offer to our community is the biggest change in our food culture that I've seen."

BUCKWHEAT CREPE CAKE

INGREDIENTS

2 cups (500 ml)	whole milk (3%)
1 Tbsp	sugar
1/4 tsp	kosher salt
80 g (3 oz)	butter, melted
70 g (2 oz)	buckwheat flour
105 g (5 oz)	all-purpose flour
3	large eggs
1 to 2 Tbsp	whole milk (3%)

TO FINISH THE DISH

1/2 cup clarified butter

Whipping cream (35%), whipped to stiff peak

Moss Berry Farm jam, as desired

METHOD

The night before, combine all ingredients and mix well to combine. Pour into a non-reactive container, cover, and allow to rest/settle/chill in fridge overnight.

Remove the batter from fridge 1 hour before use. Stir the batter briskly to loosen it up (it should be the consistency of whipping cream (35%), if it is too thick, add a tbsp of milk to loosen it up).

Heat a 8 to 9-inch (20 to 23cm) skillet on the stove over medium heat (either a seasoned crepe pan or a non-stick skillet will work best). Add a touch of clarified butter to the hot pan and swirl, or spread the melted butter using a pastry brush.

Lift the pan off the heat, add 4oz of batter to the pan, tilt and swirl the pan to distribute the batter evenly in pan, then return the pan to the heat to cook the first side of the crepe. After about 1 minute run either a non-stick spatula or an offset palette knife underneath the crepe to loosen it. Using either tool (or your fingers) flip the crepe over and continue cooking on the second side for another 30 seconds.

Continue cooking crepes until the batter has all been used, stirring the batter regularly, and stacking the cooked crepes on top of each other as you go. Cool.

TO FINISH THE DISH

Spread whipped cream and Moss Berry Farm jam onto cooled crepes, using an offset palette knife, then stack crepes on top of each other to form a multi-layered cake. Serve as desired with additional whipped cream and berries.

MIKE BOOTH

Stratford Chefs School and The Prune

Mike Booth would likely tell you that perspective is a good thing. Recalling his time as a Stratford Chefs School student, Booth acknowledges, more than a decade later, the advantage in having been taught by working chefs with different perspectives and personalities. "I realized there are many different ways to prepare and cook food. Whether or not you stir your risotto, you can still end up with great risotto," says Booth, who cooks at The Prune. He also has the perspective of starting out on an earlier career path and living in very different parts of the country. Born in B.C., his family moved to Kingsville, Ontario, in Canada's southernmost municipality, where he grew up before heading east to Sackville, New Brunswick, and a B.Sc. in chemistry at Mount Allison University. "I realized then that chemistry wasn't necessarily what I wanted to do. I like to tell my students that I didn't want to be in a white coat all day," Booth says with a wry smile. He worked in kitchens to support himself while at university; that perspective got him thinking about cooking professionally. "I did a three-month stagiaire in Italy at a one-star Michelin restaurant and spent four years in Holland. I moved back to Canada specifically to go to the Stratford Chefs School, and I basically haven't left." He graduated in 2006 and worked at Rundles until it closed operations in the fall of 2017. "It was great and difficult all at once," says Booth, who was the school's purchasing agent and is currently an instructor. "I loved it. Rundles was a fantastic

place to work. I felt really good about everything I did each day. It was about gastronomy, but your personal life suffered." Rundles' closure was difficult, he says, but it represented an evolution in the Stratford food scene. "I see a shift in the type of restaurants opening here. There's a lot more mid-level places." He has no illusions about the relationship between the restaurants and the theatre where, in summer, prix fixe menus enable kitchens to get customers fed and out the door to their show in a short window of time. It's a mercenary but realistic approach.

In his role as the school's purchasing agent, Booth dealt with farmers and appreciates the value of the relationships and the opportunity to visit the farms. "Not all chefs can do that. We'd drive out to Soiled Reputation and get stuff out of the barn and leave a note that we've taken 10 pounds of carrots." That's simple enough, yet he recognizes the complexity of farm-to-table: it's a four-month season where customers often want to come to a restaurant to have the same thing. "What do you do when it's not local fennel season, for instance?" Booth asks. Like the rule and its exception, the evolution of and the demands upon the industry are indicative of the importance of food to Stratford. "It's arts but it's also farming. It's economics. The theatre's a big thing but restaurants and farmers are getting a piece of that pie and trying to provide something additional to tourism here."

MONFORTE DAIRY

Ruth Klahsen

Not one to mince words, Ruth Klahsen describes farm-to-table as a tale of two countries. In Italy, she says, the concept is a lived behaviour where they cook and eat everything and don't really think about it. "It's simple. It's just what they do." Her experience here tells her a different story: "I'm not sure we really bought into the local thing. What really only matters to North Americans is how inexpensive their food is." Klahsen opened Monforte Dairy in Stratford in 2004, but she'd been in the city as a Stratford Chefs School graduate (1985) and a cook long before that. She describes the transition from restaurant kitchen to cheesemaker as a gradual one – and one she's reminded of seasonally. "I don't know why I picked cheese to make. It's funny, I still go past fields where you'll see animals suckling and I just smile. I have no idea what it is, but it's especially ruminants," says Klahsen. She describes Monforte as striving to be French and Italian in its artisanal approach to cheese. The bucolic picture she paints of the ideal was a sort of fantasy she once had: "Imagine you drive down the laneway to the farm and that's the cheese they're making." Pragmatically, she balances wanting Monforte's business to grow against remaining small enough to be considered artisan cheese; though it reaches Montreal and Ottawa, most of Klahsen's cheese is delivered to Toronto. Wherever it ends up, she firmly asserts that producers in Perth County need support as they evolve. "Or else, they will never get better," she says.

As both cook and cheesemaker, she states the school had a profound effect on her. "The work ethic and the information were terrific, and the way it taught you how to think and apply. It was all about the work and working hard," she emphasizes. "I'm grateful." She then points to Ryan O'Donnell at Mercer Hall as an example of the chefs the school produces today and their role in the industry. "He's really supportive of his kitchens and structures them in a way where they have support, but he also knows that his bosses need to make money. I think he's a really good example for the students and for all of us in the community." She adds that she'd like to see the school play an even greater role in building the culture of the community.

Klahsen's work – and her philosophy – is deeply rooted in the land, the seasons, sustainability, and a sense of responsibility to the animals that she relies on. "We really push hard that they're only milked seasonally so that they're dried off every year as a herd. The farmers get to rest and the animals get to rest," she says. The land, it turns out, is the reason she makes cheese. "I think Perth County has the most beautiful land in the world, but are we doing everything we should in terms of agriculture? The reason I wanted to make cheese here is because I couldn't understand why with this land we needed to import cheeses."

CHEESE BISCUITS WITH SAUSAGE GRAVY

Growing up, my mum made biscuits several times a year. We would sit down to dinner and I'd immediately reach for the basket of biscuits, still warm from the oven. Each one was torn in half and topped with butter and a drizzle of honey. There was always a basket left on the counter for later snacking. I've never known a biscuit to make it through the night.

These biscuits are great eaten any time of day, on their own or alongside a favourite meal. Recently, I have been covering them with sausage gravy and topping with a poached or fried egg making a delicious breakfast, lunch, or staff meal at the restaurant.

INGREDIENTS

CHEESE BISCUIT INGREDIENTS

2 cups	all-purpose flour
2 cups	pastry flour
1 Tbsp + 1 tsp	kosher salt
1 Tbsp	baking powder
1 tsp	baking soda
1/2 lb (227 g)	unsalted butter, cut into ¼-inch (0.6 cm) dice and frozen
1 1/2 cups	buttermilk
1/2 cup	Monforte chèvre
3/4 cup	Monforte Abondance, grated
1/4 cup	chives or green onion, thinly sliced (optional)
1/2 cup	ham, diced (optional)

METHOD

CHEESE BISCUIT

Preheat a still oven to 425F (218C).

Combine the flours, salt, baking powder and baking soda in the bowl of a food processor. Pulse to combine. Add the frozen butter, and pulse until it is roughly the size of lentils (sandy/gravely). Remove to a large mixing bowl.

Meanwhile, in a separate mixing bowl, slowly add the buttermilk to the chèvre, using a spatula to combine the two. The mixture should be very thick at first and end up pourable. If it is a little lumpy, that is fine.

Make a well in the centre of the flour mixture. Sprinkle the grated cheese and optional ingredients (if using) over the flour mixture. Add the buttermilk mixture to the centre of the flour well, and fold together using a fork, or wooden spoon. The dough should begin to come together, but not form a solid mass. Do not overwork the dough, or the biscuits will be tough.

Turn the dough out onto a lightly floured work surface, and using your fingers, pat into a rectangle about ¾-inches (2 cm) thick, slightly larger than a standard sheet of paper.

I like to cut my biscuits with a knife, into square(ish) pieces. I yield 12 large, or 18 smaller biscuits from this recipe. If you like round biscuits, cut with a 2-1/2-inch (6 cm) ring cutter or drinking glass. The excess dough can be pushed back together and cut again.

Place the biscuits 2-inches apart on a baking sheet lined with parchment paper. Bake in your preheated oven for 18-25 minutes (depending on the size you cut). Remove from the oven to a wire cooling rack. Serve warm.

SAUSAGE GRAVY INGREDIENTS

1 Tbsp	vegetable oil
1 lb (454 g)	sausage meat - you can make this (recipe follows), or use your favourite store bought version
1/3 cup	all-purpose flour
4 cups (1 L)	whole milk (3%)
1/2 tsp	kosher salt, more to taste
2 tsp	freshly ground black pepper
1/8 tsp	celery salt
5 dashes	Tabasco
2 tsp	Maggi seasoning, or Worcestershire sauce, more to taste

METHOD

SAUSAGE GRAVY METHOD

Warm a large, heavy skillet over medium heat. Add the vegetable oil and sausage meat, trying to break the sausage up, with a spoon, into bite-sized pieces as it cooks. Brown the sausage evenly until it is no longer pink. Remove the cooked sausage to a bowl.

Reduce the heat to medium-low. Sprinkle in half of the flour and stir so that it combines with the residual sausage fat. Slowly add the remaining flour, little by little, stirring constantly. Cook the flour for a minute or two, then begin adding the milk in 1 cup (250 ml) increments, stirring constantly. If you add the milk all at once, your gravy will be lumpy.

When all of the milk has been incorporated, return the sausage meat to the skillet and add the salt, pepper and other seasonings. Simmer the gravy, stirring often, until it thickens (about 10 to 15 minutes). If the gravy seems to be getting too thick, simply add a little more milk. Taste, and adjust the seasoning as required.

SAUSAGE INGREDIENTS

900 g (32 oz)	boneless pork shoulder, diced into 1-inch pieces
227 g (8 oz)	pork back fat, diced into 1-inch pieces
20 g (0.7 oz)	kosher salt
16 g (0.6 oz)	sugar
6 g (0.2 oz)	garlic, minced
8 g (0.3 oz)	fennel seeds, toasted
3 g (0.1 oz)	black pepper, coarsely ground
5 g (0.2 oz)	chilli flakes
6 g (0.2 oz)	Spanish paprika
1/3 cup	ice water
2 Tbsp	red wine vinegar, chilled

METHOD

SAUSAGE METHOD

Combine the first 9 ingredients in a large mixing bowl and toss to evenly distribute the seasonings. Refrigerate until ready to grind.

Grind the mixture through a meat grinder with a medium/small die attachment. Pass half of the mixture through the meat grinder a second time (this will help to bind the mixture while leaving some texture).

Place the sausage mixture in the bowl of a stand mixer fitted with the paddle attachment. Mix on medium speed while slowly pouring in the cold water and vinegar. Continue mixing until the sausage has a uniform, sticky consistency.

Pan-fry a small piece of sausage meat and adjust for seasoning as required.

RANDI RUDNER

Stratford Chefs School And Pazzo Taverna

Growing up in Montreal and attending Queen's University in Kingston offered Randi Rudner both a view of a world-class cosmopolitan city and education in philosophy and classics. "I was interested in pursuing law or medicine and my parents were also highly interested in my pursuing law or medicine," she says, tongue-in-cheek. However, in an existential way, Kierkegaard and Greco-Roman antiquities qualified her to serve fries and sling beer to earn a living: she eventually got kitchen work in a Kingston restaurant run by graduates of the Stratford Chefs School. "I sort of fell into it," Rudner says. Formerly of Rundles, she's worked at Pazzo Taverna with chef Yva Santini, and she manages the Chefs School program and is teaches in both the classroom and the kitchen. Add to that her work on school administration, supporting governance policy, scheduling, guidance, and report cards, and it makes for a few different hats for Rudner to wear.

Her graduation from Stratford in 2011 represented a second career path, if not exactly a second career. But the pattern of switching direction is something she's observed frequently, both in her kitchen work and teaching experience. "I think in a lot of ways, the school is really responding to the reality that this is a second career for a lot of people, or that being a chef is not an ultimate goal. It can open a lot of different doors," says Rudner. What she's also observed – and what informs her teaching – is that feeding people is an honourable profession. "It's satisfying to do this noble thing every day with excellence, discipline, and integrity in the kitchen. That's part of the school's mandate." But so too is addressing the more problematic side of the restaurant industry. "It historically has not always been a healthy environment for anybody, not just women. It can be equally oppressive to men," Rudner stresses. "So I think mentoring students to demand and create a better and more respectful workplace is one of the most important things we do at the school."

As a member of the teaching staff and school administration, Rudner sees the school as part of an evolving network that makes it unique. "The producers here grew along with the city and the restaurants and the school," Rudner says, describing how instructors and students might work with a producer in meal prep during the day and then that producer visits for the meal that night. They learn about exotic ingredients not part of our northern climate and about local produce in their own backyard: Perth County beets and pork belly or Lake Huron perch. "I think we are incredibly lucky at the school to be able to do what we do with the students we work with and the quality of alumni and producers that support us," Rudner says. "On any given night during the school season, Antony John or Max Lass might be in the dining room. It's a supportive community, and we're all working in the service of eating better."

REVEL

Anne Campion

At least part of the credo that grounds the team that owns and operates revel is "Independent Coffee for a Revolution." The tagline found on their website, possessed of seemingly weighty concepts, simply encourages one to re-think the connection between food and community. "My goal when we purchased revel eight years ago was to be for the good of our community, both locally and globally," says revel owner Anne Campion, adding that virtually everything at the Market Place café starts with relationships. In the store itself, among its 19 employees, she says mutual respect and looking out for each other is paramount. "That enables us to look outward to our community and make revel a welcoming place to anyone who visits." The philosophy then extends to the food and beverage at the café where Chef Jordan Lassaline sources ingredients and products from the area, Campion says. "We're asking, how are they growing things sustainably here and in a relationship with the earth?" Further afield, literally thousands of kilometres away where sourcing coffee is problematic, the question is the same. Revel focuses on relationships there, too: every coffee bean they purchase must be part of what Campion calls "a relationship" – and that means, she says, not just fair trade, but direct trade. "We're building relationships with farmers and the small micro-roasters that we have chosen to work with." Currently, revel is working primarily with Latin American farmers because there is better traceability and transparency,

she says. "If I want to have a sustainable way of living, then I have to know that the person who is growing the coffee beans we serve is able to have that as well. Our community starts with direct trade with the coffee farmer. Everything else on our menu that doesn't come from our region has to be sourced equitably and sustainably."

Among business relationships, revel has partnerships with Red Rabbit and Okazu, The Prune and Mercer Hall, the new vegan restaurant Grounded, and the Stratford Chefs School. "We know the stories about locally raised meat, the vegetables that are grown organically, and the VQA wines that are available on restaurant menus, but coffee comes as the throw-away at the end of the meal. We're excited that there are restaurants and the Chefs School in our community, many of whom have said they want to be part of our approach and have chosen us as a coffee partner." In fact, Campion, along with her husband Dave Campion, a Stratford Festival musician, have been visiting the school for 30 years. "I think what's exciting for me is that it goes back to those relationships. The instructors help create culinary expertise but also chefs who will go across Canada and ask, what food in this specific region can I be highlighting? Who are the farmers that I could be building relationships with? The school invites students to do that," she says. "We've always had Chefs School students in our business. Together we have respect for our food."

COFFEE-ROASTED CARROTS WITH RED-EYE MISO GRAVY

Anne Campion's approach to coffee is an inspiration to me, and having worked as her pastry chef at revel some years ago, I have come to appreciate the role coffee can play as a partner at the table. Not just in desserts or as an after-dinner beverage, mind you—the range of Anne's meticulously sourced and roasted coffee beans work beautifully in the savoury kitchen, and can bring unexpected earthy, floral, and even fruity notes to the table.

The anchor of this dish, the carrots roasted in whole coffee beans, is adapted from a recipe by Daniel Patterson, of Coi restaurant in San Francisco. Coi pairs the carrots with a light sauce made of bright and fresh mandarin orange juice, as a pre-dessert palate cleanser, but these carrots are equally at home with this heavier, more robust sauce. I like to roast carrots in revel's Marketplace coffee beans, which is a Nicaraguan single origin, honey-washed caturra bean. In the cup, Marketplace unmistakably expresses blueberries, and in this preparation on the plate, the coffee adds a fruitiness that complements the sweet carrots, in addition to the coffee flavour you would expect. Choosing great carrots is also important to the success of this recipe; I have the great privilege of working with Antony John's carrots from Soiled Reputation farm. Antony's carrots are so sweet and perfect, and they are available from his root cellar well into the winter; in fact, winter carrots are even sweeter than the first baby carrots available in high summer (although those are hard to resist!)

Red-eye gravy is a traditional Southern sauce made of Country ham drippings and black coffee. Replacing the ham grease with white miso, a Japanese paste of fermented soybeans, makes for a lighter, vegetarian sauce, which still packs an umami punch. The coffee should be on the stronger side, but not so bracing as a shot of espresso. I like to use Don Rey's Private Reserve (Continental Roast) from revel, which is rich, smokey, and chocolatey. It is my favourite of all the coffees at revel, and it is what I drink every morning. Use whatever you've got on hand; according to tradition, Red-eye gravy is made with cold, leftover coffee.

This would be a good side dish for a larger meal, or could be a satisfying lunch with a softly poached egg on top (and a slice of crusty bread to mop up the gravy and egg!)

Serves 4 as a side dish, or 2 as a more substantial plate

INGREDIENTS

FOR THE CARROTS

1 lb (454 g)	thin, multicolour carrots from Soiled Reputation. Buy local, buy seasonal, buy organic. If you can get your hands on Antony John's round Thumbelina carrots, those are exceptional too!
1 Tbsp	vegetable oil
	kosher salt and freshly ground black pepper to taste
3/4 lb (340 g)	whole revel Marketplace coffee beans

FOR THE GRAVY

1	medium onion, finely diced
2 Tbsp	unsalted butter
2 Tbsp	vegetable oil
	kosher salt and freshly ground black pepper to taste
2 Tbsp	all-purpose flour
1 cup (250 ml)	strong brewed Don Rey's Private Reserve coffee
1 Tbsp	white miso vigorously whisked with 2 tablespoons water to produce a smooth paste
	fresh lemon juice to taste

TO SERVE

2 handfuls of Soiled Reputation mizuna, wild arugula or another spicy green

1 poached egg per person, if desired

Crusty bread, if desired

METHOD

THE CARROTS

Preheat a still oven to 350F (180C).

Scrub the carrots well, but do not peel them. Coat them with the vegetable oil, and season with salt and pepper. Spread half the coffee beans in a roasting pan just large enough to accommodate all the carrots in a single layer. Lay the carrots over top of the beans, and cover with the remaining half of the coffee beans. Put the pan in the oven, uncovered, and roast until the carrots are perfectly tender. Make sure that the carrots are completely cooked—as they roast, they will express their sweetness, which is a foil to the aromatic coffee beans surrounding and infusing them. The amount of time this takes will depend on the kind of carrots you end up with—the best way to gauge doneness is to pierce a carrot with a skewer or the tip of a knife, and assess its texture.

PS: you probably won't want to brew your morning coffee with the beans you used to roast the carrots, but you certainly can reuse them a second, and even a third time for the same recipe! Just let them cool, and store them in a cool, dark place (or in the freezer), in an airtight container.

THE GRAVY

Sweat the diced onion in the butter and oil in a heavy-bottomed saucepan over medium-low heat. Season very lightly with salt, and quite liberally with freshly ground black pepper. Go slow—it takes longer to properly cook an onion than you might think, and you want to coax sweetness out of it. Once the onion is completely soft and golden, you can turn the heat up and let the onion take on some deeper colour. Once the onion is a pleasant light caramel colour, add the flour to the pan, and stir to coat the onion. Stirring constantly, cook out the flour for a minute or two, to avoid a raw, floury taste in your finished sauce. Mind that the flour doesn't catch and burn. Deglaze the pan with the coffee, using a wooden spoon or spatula to scrape up any stuck bits of onion. Whisk in the miso/water mixture. Simmer over medium-high heat until thickened. At this point, you could blend the gravy if the small bits of onion offend you, but I am inclined to leave it as is. Check for seasoning, adding salt or pepper as necessary, and finish with lemon juice to taste.

TO SERVE

Warm the cooked carrots in a low oven or in a pan on the stovetop, and once hot, toss with the mizuna off the heat. Drizzle with the hot gravy, and top with a poached egg, if desired. Serve with crusty bread on the side, if you wish!

BRYAN STEELE

Stratford Chefs School

Born in Témiscaming, Quebec, about 500 km due north of Toronto, Bryan Steele hadn't planned on being a cook, but, like many chefs, he made the transition from a career path that was unrelated to cooking. After his third year of studying life sciences and biochemistry at Queen's University in Kingston, Ontario, he said the subject just didn't resonate with him. "I wasn't sure what I was going to do and where all of it was going to take me." Steele completed the degree, but that summer he applied for kitchen work at the Windsor Arms Hotel and Four Seasons Hotel Toronto. Luck was with him: "I got interviews for both, although neither had openings right away. I just loved the fact that both were really cool spots, and I just loved the idea of cooking." A month later, Steele was in the Windsor Arms kitchen and would soon be attending George Brown College for culinary training. He eventually found himself at Scaramouche – with only three years cooking experience – being mentored by Canadian culinary icons Michael Stadtlander and Jamie Kennedy. Soon after, he was in Verona, Italy, and from there did a stagiaire in Schwäbisch Gmünd, Germany, at Vincent Klink's 40-seat, Michelin-starred restaurant,

Postillon, eventually becoming sous chef. "I had intended on staying in Germany for only one year, but through various connections I developed it evolved into five years cooking in Europe."

The road to Stratford and the Chefs School was just ahead. In the late 1980s, Steele had what he still calls "one the greatest conversations I have ever had about food" with SCS co-founder Eleanor Kane. Steele became chef at The Old Prune and started teaching practical culinary classes at the school, a role he has held for decades.

One focus that he says is key for culinary students is appreciating the importance of taste. "I find that young chefs need to appreciate that right off the bat. Sometimes I think that they believe the visual aesthetic should supersede that. It's easy to be seduced by the visual and while I like simple and beautiful presentation, taste is often given short shrift." Steele says that "people's interest in becoming professional cooks has expanded exponentially" and that culinary education must meet that appetite. "There's a new educated and savvy dining public which demands more of cooks," he says. "More than ever, those cooks need a greater knowledge base."

FRANCES LATHAM

Stratford Chefs School

Like many of her colleagues, Frances Latham's appearance in the kitchens at the Stratford Chefs School in 1989 marked the beginning of a second career. Having spent time in the corporate world, she decided she'd had enough of typical office dynamics. "I just thought, I can't do this any longer," says Latham. She learned of the School through Chris Woolf, now chef and restaurateur at Little Red's in St. Marys and formerly an instructor at the school. "Food and wine were big in my life, so I decided to check it out. I eventually got to work for a summer at Rundles. I only wish I had discovered the food-service industry earlier." Now in her third year of teaching students front-of-house service, she operated Smith and Latham in St. Marys with business partner Robert Smith, a former pastry instructor at the School. Her husband, Bob Latham, now Sommelier and wine instructor at the School, was sponsored by Smith and Latham to become a Sommelier and run the wine program at the restaurant. "We ran the restaurant from 1995 to 2008. That's a long time," Latham says. "Our girls grew up there." In her first term at the School, there weren't many students compared to today, which has allowed her to observe the institution's steady growth and community building that was far different then. "It was the wild west here. Everyone had great passion, as I'm sure they do today, but things were less structured. I gained a great knowledge base, but you did have to learn in a different way."

Looking across the larger industry now, she describes Stratford and Perth County as something akin to a tale of two cities, but many customers are indeed asking more about where their food comes from and how it was produced. "You can see improvement in the mainstream food industry," she says. "It's becoming a very rich food and dining culture." She attributes that fact in part to the Chefs School's presence and its growth. Even as a small program, she says it has "pushed the boundaries of culinary education" producing talented cooks for finer dining and instilling entrepreneurial spirit in graduates to open fantastic restaurants. "The school has developed a good reputation and people want to come into the trade at this high level," according to Latham. At the same time, she's realistic about how tough the industry is and the challenges it faces. "There are some things we can't do," she says. The example extends to virtually all restaurateurs in an industry with razor thin margins and limited resources. Yet, within constraints there can be opportunity: it might be relatively easy to cook with an excellent ingredient, but the trick, Latham suggests, is being able to create inventive and delicious food using any cut of meat, for instance. "That's the reality," she says. "Most of the students go out to work in restaurants where there is never enough money to work with. You have to be creative and apply good techniques and respect the integrity of the ingredients that you have."

KATHY BELL

Stratford Chefs School and Keystone Alley

Kathy Bell had always enjoyed cooking casually, but she moved into the industry professionally after having spent several years in the medical field. She grew up about 20 minutes from Stratford in St. Marys, Ontario, and after high school she trained as an x-ray technician. One thing led to another, and she was soon living in Toronto where she worked for about a decade. "I was in a small community clinic at Dufferin and St. Clair, but I just wanted more I guess," Bell says. To help make a decision about her future direction, Bell took some career counselling – it determined she liked working with her hands, and that finding melded nicely with the fact that she had always liked to cook. She enrolled in the George Brown culinary program and attended her first year, but that summer a visit to Stratford's Prune restaurant led to a serendipitous conversation with Stratford artist and designer Kato Wake during which she learned that there was a culinary school starting up in the city; Wake encouraged her to apply. "I went to an interview with Eleanor [Kane], and then quickly withdrew from George Brown, moved back home, started at the school, and became an apprentice. It all happened within a very short time," she says. Bell was part of the first graduating class of the school. She logged 30 years – a period she defines as "a very long time" as dining room manager at Rundles restaurant before she moved to the front of the house at Keystone Alley last year. "It's a totally different experience," she says of the two restaurants.

Bell has been involved with and taught at the school in various capacities, starting as a Purchasing Instructor. Regarding work and employment issues in the industry, Bell has noticed a positive evolution in that span of time. "The work hours have changed dramatically. I remember 14-hour days six days a week. That's different now," she says. What she says hasn't changed has been the essence of the Chefs School's mandate: to offer high-quality cookery instruction, stimulate entrepreneurial spirit, and encourage innovation in its students. Bell says that much of the success that the school has had in meeting that mandate – with only 70 or so students – is its relatively small size. "I like how small the school is. That's unique. Students are on a first-name basis and there are fewer barriers between students and faculty. It gives it a close, family dynamic," she says. That closeness and personal touch applies to the school's suppliers and those of the restaurants in the area too. "Knowing your suppliers on a first-name basis is quite important," she says, adding that customers, increasingly, are asking more frequently where their food comes from. "A customer came in the other day and asked me to tell him about the salmon. The consumer has prompted a response and is much better informed."

NEIL BAXTER

Stratford Chefs School And Weekend Cooking Class Retreats

With the closure of Rundles in late 2017, SCS senior cookery instructor Neil Baxter was suddenly a chef in search of a kitchen – but he's in no particular hurry. "Ask me next year if I want to cook," he says. "It's been 35 years since I've enjoyed a summer outside of Stratford. I was in Brampton the other night, and I thought to myself that this is Saturday at 6 o'clock and I'm dining in a restaurant. It was odd." Scottish-born, Baxter travelled with his family whose father was in the Royal Navy. They eventually settled in Cheltenham, characterized by the rolling hills and verdant walkways of the south-central Gloucestershire Cotswolds. There, he attended culinary school and did his apprenticeship. "In the early 1980s, I sent applications for work to South Africa and Australia. I also sent one to Rundles restaurant, even though I had no idea who Rundles restaurant was. I was nervous when I met with Jim Morris. He said I was either very good or very bad. I think he opted for very good, and I came here in the summer of 1981." Soon after, stagiaires sent Baxter travelling again: to Quilted Giraffe, New York; Troisgros, Lyon; Tour d'Argent, Paris; and to Chez Panisse with Paul Bertolli. "By that time, the school had started. I joined in the second year as an instructor and was chef at Rundles. Prior to my coming here, the three main restaurants were The Church, The Old Prune, and Rundles. Before that, there was nothing here offering that kind of food and dining."

Baxter's reflections on the school and the food scene, understandably, derive out of his Rundles' tenure. "In those days, the school was a fledgling organization trying to find footing in food education. It evolved from 12 people and it's grown significantly from there. Walk into almost any restaurant in Stratford, and you're going to find either a chef in charge of the kitchen or a manager or front-of-house staff who have come through the school. We've had a lot of graduates who've gone on to do good things, whether they stayed in the kitchen, opened a bakery, or started making cheese. The catalyst came from Jim and Eleanor." Baxter speculates about how Rundles would have evolved as a 12-month restaurant. "As it was, it was hard to develop the structure of supplies for a short period of time. We always had a prix fixe menu and always needed product on hand and used the suppliers here as much as we could. But we closed for the season just when late summer and fall produce was available." Despite Rundles' closure and the dissolution of the team – "when you have a strong relationship with strong people you can trust, it's sad to see it go" – Stratford will evolve and continue to adjust to the market, he says. "I don't think you can say that the food scene in Stratford has not been influenced by the school and will continue to be. The school, the food scene, and the theatre are very closely linked. Stratford is a special place."

ABOUT THE AUTHOR

ANDREW COPPOLINO

Andrew Coppolino is a Kitchener-based writer and broadcaster and is food columnist with the Kitchener Post and CBC Radio in Waterloo Region. He is a past instructor at the Stratford Chefs School and a former restaurant reviewer for the Waterloo Region Record. He holds a Master's degree in English literature from the University of Waterloo. Coppolino is co-author of Cooking with Shakespeare (Greenwood Press) and has published in newspapers and magazines across Canada, and in the United States and England. Following a stint as an apprentice chef at 20 King Restaurant in Kitchener, Coppolino chose to work with food from the other side of the kitchen pass. As a food writer, he has been dedicated to promoting and nurturing culinary businesses and advocating for the chefs and restaurants in Waterloo Region and the nearby cities of Guelph and Stratford. As a de facto ambassador for local food, he believes a strong food landscape requires imaginative and technically proficient cooks, creative and forward-looking restaurants, and consumers who are knowledgeable about the art, craft, and economics of the industry. When he isn't writing about food, Coppolino is very likely eating it.

ABOUT THE PHOTOGRAPHER

TERRY MANZO

A client once said, "I wish I could see the world through your eyes."

Terry Manzo has been a professional freelance photographer for thirty years. Her photographs combine unique and compelling perspectives with strong technical skills. She has exhibited regularly in Ontario and worked on several ambitious social media projects, posting daily or weekly photographs or photographic collages for a year during 2011, 2013, and 2016. Many in the Stratford area know and respect her for the photography courses she has been teaching at Gallery Stratford since 1999. Her commercial work encompasses a broad spectrum from publicity, events, products, concerts, and theatre, to people at work and play.

As photographer for the Stratford Chefs School, Terry's delectable food shots and vibrant event coverage contribute to its world class reputation. Terry is a Stratford Chefs School Alumni, graduating in the inaugural class of 1985.

ABOUT SWAN PARADE PRESS

Swan Parade PRESS

Swan Parade Press, an imprint of Blue Moon Publishers, carefully curates a list of books that are driven by regionally based voices and perspectives. This regional imprint features contemporary and historic stories of Stratford and surrounding areas in many literary forms, such as novels and memoirs, as well as broad non-fiction titles such as cookbooks and travel guides. It is our goal to identify the many dimensions of our region so locals and visitors alike can deepen their understanding of this unique and diverse community that spans from the arts to agriculture.

We welcome submissions directed to Swan Parade Press via the guidelines on our website:

www.bluemoonpublishers.com.

ACKNOWLEDGMENTS

FROM STRATFORD CHEFS SCHOOL

Our **Co-founders** for their vision, passion, creativity, tenacity, and spirit.

Our volunteer **Board of Directors** for their tireless dedication, knowledge, guidance, and support; Ryan Donovan*, Nigel Howard, Timothy J. Leonard, Dr. Dennis Nuhn, David Stones, and Kathy Vassilakos.

Our **Advisory Group** for their commitment, enthusiasm, time, and generosity; Dan Donovan*, Carl Heinrich*, Eleanor Kane, Rick Matthews, Jessie Votary, and Carrie Wreford.

Our **Team** whose energy, dedication, heart, and skill make our day-to-day accomplishments possible; Theresa Albert, Neil Baxter, Kathy Bell*, Mike Booth*, Simon Briggs*, Marc Chartrand*, Robert Friesen*, Melissa Graham, Herb Hartfiel, Matthew Hartney*, Tamara Kucheran, Bob Latham,

Frances Latham*, Ian Middleton*, Erin Negus*, Randi Runder*, Eli Silverthorne*, Stepfanie Spencer*, Bryan Steele, Margaret Strawbridge, Aurelia Szilagi, and LeCinda Walker.

Our new **Alumni Association Committee** who work diligently to undertake initiatives to improve the experiences of our students and alumni; Mel Athulathmudali*, Donna Borooah*, Ryan Donovan*, Jessica Iveson*, Kaya Ogruce*, David Stones and Brandon Wraith*.

Alumni Guest Chef Mentors (in addition to those already mentioned in this book!) who work with our students throughout the year at various classes and events; Rocco Agostino*, Francisco Alejandri*, Charmaine Baan*, Ryan Brown*, Ryan Crawford*, Jeff Crump*, Ryan Donovan*, Allison Howard*, Heidi Noble*, Eric Neaves*, Kaya Ogruce*, Jeff Sample*, Kiki Sontiyart*, Cameron Stauch*, Erin Turcke*, and James Walt*.

Our valued **Partners**; Anne & Dave Campion, Andrew Coppolino, Black Swan Brewing Co., Bradshaws & Kitchen Detail, Cave Spring Cellars, Church Hill Farm, The City of Stratford & Mayor Dan Mathieson, Creative Feats & Heidi Holdsworth, DigiWriting Team Members & Heidi Sander, Downie Street Bakehouse, Employment Ontario, Farm Juice Co., Gail Tolley, Hooked*, Joseph Hoare Gastronomic Writer in Residence Committee, John Wolfe, Loco Fields, Max and Vicki Lass, McIntosh Farms, The Milkey Whey, Monforte Dairy* & Ruth Klahsen*, Ontario Ministry of Training Colleges and Universities, Perth Pork Products, revel, Soiled Reputation & Antony John, Stratford Festival, Stratford Tourism Alliance, Stuart Arkett, Swan Parade Press, Tea Leaves & Karen Hartwick, Terry Manzo*, The Three Houses & David Lester, and The Vine Agency.

Our generous **Sponsors**; Elizabeth Baird, BMO Financial Group, Sylvia Chrominska, Dr. Robert Close, Garland Canada A Welbilt Company, Dr. Dennis & Laurie Nuhn, Sandra and Jim Pitblado, RE/MAX a-b Realty Ltd., and Richmond Station*. And thank you to the Ontario Ministry of Agriculture, Food and Rural Affairs for providing funding toward *Farm to Table* in order to complete the production of this book.

A special thank you to all members of our community who help to make our student success stories possible; accommodation providers, dinner patrons, employers, and donors.

*SCS alumni or alumni owned business

STRATFORD
CHEFS
SCHOOL

ACKNOWLEDGMENTS

FROM ANDREW COPPOLINO

Thank you to Blue Moon Publishers and to the Stratford Chefs School for the opportunity to participate in this project which, I hope, captures an important part of the food and culinary essence of Perth and Huron counties.

To Peter Martin for the opportunity to cook at his 20 King Restaurant, and to Chef Lori Maidlow for teaching me the basics in that kitchen. It helped me to see how rewarding – and demanding – the craft is. Though it wasn't the plan, it also opened the door for me to do what I love doing today: exploring and writing about food.

And, of course, a book with "farm to table" in its title would not have been possible were it not for the talented and inventive chefs, farmers, and producers who are part of our `communities. Your dedication to all kinds of good food is inspiring – and delicious.